Notes from Ivory Flats

Reflections on the changing landscape of academic life

Robert Foley

Cam Rivers Publishing

First English Edition Published in Great Britain

By CAM RIVERS PUBLISHING LTD 2024

NOTES FROM IVORY FLATS
REFLECTIONS ON THE CHANGING LANDSCAPE OF ACADEMIC LIFE

Author: Robert Foley

Honorary Editor: Professor Alan Macfarlane FBA
Editor-in-Chief: WANG Zilan
Editor: Irene Galstian, QIN Yuchen

Cover Design: GE Dalong (MUYE)
Design and Typeset: QIN Yubin(MUYE)

The publishing of this book is supported by
the Vanishing Worlds Foundation, U.K.

A CIP Catalogue of this book is available from the British Library

ISBN: 978-1-916858-67-1

Contact: press@cambridgerivers.com
www.cambridgerivers.com

For all the wonderful friends, colleagues, and students from Cambridge and all over the world that, despite everything, make academic life, and life more generally, so pleasurable.

PREFACE

Academics are prone to grumbling. And there are many things to grumble about. Our books and papers that are not appreciated as they should be, students who fail to laugh at our jokes, heads of departments who want us to move into smaller offices, administrators who think an empty diary is a sign of inactivity, and, of course, governments who persistently pare higher education down to the bone.

Notes from Ivory Flats began life as grumbles with colleagues and friends in the pub over a beer or glass of wine, often after a particularly onerous or boring meeting, or across a wider network at conferences. Eventually, bored with my own grumbles, I decided to write about them, and this book is the result. They also morphed from being grumbles to a more reflective view on life in a modern university from the point of view of academic staff, the foot soldiers of teaching and research.

The reflections that follow were first published in the *Oxford Magazine*, and I would like to thank its editors, especially Tim Horder, for encouraging me to do so. Various people read drafts of some of them, and provided helpful comments and advice — especially Hugh Foley and Jonathan Goodman. Marta Mirazón Lahr read all of them, and made sure I kept the tone light and the focus sharp, and, as always, I am endlessly grateful to her.

List Of Contents

1

A CHANGE OF ADDRESS

The landscape stretched away into the distance, a patchwork of fields of contrasting greens, cosy villages and sprawling brown-grey towns. Dotted across this landscape were white towers, stretching up to meet the blue skies. These ivory towers sparkled in the sun, with light glinting from their facetted surfaces.

At the tops of these towers, small black-dressed figures could be seen gesticulating, chattering, and their wine glasses flashed in the sun as they sipped steadfastly. In the afternoon light, an aura of wisdom and knowledge seemed to radiate from these towers.

Then, from the north, a cold wind began to blow, bringing dark clouds across the blue sky, through which only a few stray rays could penetrate. Eventually the whole sky was grey and ominous. The clouds seemed to get lower, until they merged with the fogs that were rising up from the ground. First the fields and woods disappeared, then the villages and towns, until finally all that was left between land and sky were the white ivory towers. But the fogs and mists rose further, until they too disappeared.

The day ended, and the night passed, and with the morning came the sun again. The greens and browns of the land reappeared, the rural and urban quilt returned. But the ivory towers were now gone, and in their place were white blocks of buildings, radiating their fake plastic ivory cladding. Behind the windows, row upon row of figures could be seen at desks, faces glowing in the reflected light of their computer screens. On the closest one a large neon sign could be seen '**Welcome to Ivory Flats — universities for the twenty-first century**'.

A rather overblown metaphor, of course, but where academic life was once blithely characterised as 'living in an Ivory Tower', it is now a much more down-sized and constrained world. As long as I have been an academic — my first post was in 1977 — it has always been hard and committed work, but there is no doubt that the level of stress, intensity and pressure from all around — economics, governments, administrators, department heads, vice-chancellors, students — is immeasurably greater. The waves of strikes, mental health issues, and the trend of people abandoning academic life are evidence that all is not well in the UK university system. While much of the public debate has been about the welfare of students, and the epidemic of mental health issues among them is testament to the significance of this, much less has been said about the impact of these pressures on the academics who must deliver the teaching and keep the coffers of the universities full by attracting students and research grants.

These short pieces are reflections on how the move from our Ivory Towers to Ivory Flats (Apartments for non-Brits) has changed the lives of academics. Of course, there never really were ivory towers, not even metaphorical ones, and universities have always been well rooted in the lives and work of the people and institutions among which they exist. But the contrast between ivory towers and the modern mundane flats is itself a useful metaphor for the changes that have taken place over the last thirty years or more.

In 1908 another Cambridge academic, Francis Cornford published his *Microcosmographia*[1], a short guide to academic politics. It became a renowned pamphlet, with its 'Principle of the Wedge' ('that you should not act justly now for fear of raising expectations that you may act still more justly in the future — expectations which you are afraid you will not have the courage to satisfy') and the 'The Principle of the Dangerous Precedent' ('you should not now do an admittedly right action for fear you, or your equally timid successors, should not have the courage to do right in some future case').

Cornford was writing at a time when change in Cambridge was glacial at best, and he focused on identifying all the ways in which astute and conservative academics found ways to thwart reforms. To some extent, *Notes from Ivory Flats* is a *Microcosmographia* for the twenty-first century, but with a difference. Where Cornford was concerned with the slow pace of change at the beginning of the twentieth century, I am concerned not so much with the pace of change, but its direction, and who or what is driving that change. And where Cornford wrote about academic politics, I have written more broadly about life in academia — indeed, there is very little politics here. As a result, these pieces — hopefully written in the same relatively light-hearted vein as Cornford's book — focus more on how to resist some of the more unfortunate shifts there have been in the last few decades.

The bulk of my career was during a period when there was far less pressure and far fewer restraints and constraints on academics. For most of the time, I do not remember being very concerned about 'the authorities' and what they might expect us to do, or even being told much what to do.

I also spent most of my career in Cambridge, one of the least centralised universities, well-resourced for teaching and research, and surrounded by supportive colleagues and administrators. But if I, at the top of one of the best resourced universities, began to feel the heat as this century developed, then imagine what it must be like for those at the start of their careers and in more precarious positions.

Like Cornford's book, my reflections are inevitably primarily about how I have experienced changes in Cambridge (well, to be more precise, his book was more about how he did not experience change in Cambridge). That experience must colour what I have written, but I hope that I have managed to find themes that go well beyond Cambridge, or Oxbridge more generally, and capture the zeitgeist of academic life in the UK more generally.

What are the differences between now and the beginning of my career? Since that is now nearly fifty years ago, the memories may be a bit out of focus, and perhaps there is a touch of rose-tinted spectacles distorting them. But, while it wasn't a utopia, it certainly had advantages at an individual level.

Looking back, and comparing it with the life of early career researchers today, perhaps the biggest difference is that the move from PhD to some level of job security was much more rapid. In those days, it was not unusual to go from the PhD straight into a permanent lectureship, or at least after only one postdoctoral position. This had many consequences — one grew up academically much faster, gained independence sooner, and acquired the security necessary to take risks. Not to mention, buy a house and start a family before middle age set in.

Now, the early career researcher is likely to go from one postdoc to another, reaching their thirties while still, in a way, an apprentice (or considered to be one).

Perhaps related to that greater security was much less pressure. You were expected to do all the things you were supposed to do, but not necessarily on a short timescale — the book gestated over a few years, not pumping out multiple journal papers. And that gave time to think, to learn new things, above all, explore the intellectual and scientific universe about you.

Personally, I felt little pressure from 'above', so that pressure was more about wanting to gain respect from colleagues, or just doing well for yourself. This resulted in a much more inwardly driven career, whereas now it is all about performing for others, indeed, performing for 'them'. It is now more performing seal than lion roaming the intellectual jungle.

And, of course, there was just much less 'stuff'. Universities are about teaching and research, and that is what academics are supposed to do. But looking now at how people actually spend their time, I see that, while they may be doing things that are related to teaching and research, it is seldom direct action — not lecturing, but uploading powerpoints, not researching, but filling in risk asessments or writing yet another grant proposal... and so it goes.

These ideas are filled out in this book, a personal mapping of how university life for lecturers and professors has morphed from a slightly anarchic world where individuals pursued their dreams of finding out things and passing the torch to new generations, to a more corporate and institutionally focused one — Ivory Flats, not Ivory Towers.

It might seem that more than forty years have instilled a cynicism in me, and a loss of love for the world in which I have worked. There has certainly been a loss of innocence, but that is all. Most academics — myself included — pursue a career in universities because we love the research, enjoy and are rewarded by teaching and mentoring, and find great satisfaction in building our institutions. The surprising thing, given what you are about to read, is that I still feel that way, but in a way that is much more suspicious of the management of the institutions, and sadder about the future for younger colleagues. I am far from being one of Cornford's 'Non-Placets' (it does not please me) who oppose all change; indeed, in my career I have usually been in the vanguard of change. But when change undermines and even destroys what makes a university a great place to study and work, then a bit of resistance is no bad thing.

Students play little part in these reflections, and that may seem odd in a book about university life. While there have been shifts in the relationships between students and their lecturers, and certainly greater expectations on their part, to some extent they are a constant — wonderful and exasperating as they always have been. Although we all can moan about some of the demands they can make (or indeed, their absences and lack of demands) — they are not the focus of the discontent I describe here. Our concerns lie upwards and into the centre of our institutions, not with the student body.

These reflections, which are far from rigorous or systematic analyses of the situation (and hopefully more readable for that!), are not written to change the world or to turn the clock back — as Louis MacNeice wrote, 'you can break the bloody glass, but you can't hold up the weather' — but to think about how different academic life is now from when I first started, what has been lost, perhaps what has been gained, and what might be restored.

I have been particularly struck recently by my belated recognition that younger academics know no other world than the managerial, centralised, top-down one in which they have grown up, and things that to me seem extraordinary, they, in contrast, find quite normal.

This normalisation is natural and inevitable, just as no doubt the normal that I grew up with would have seemed strange and different to earlier generations. Each of us finds normal the world we are used to, even if there may once have been other worlds. So, these pieces are simply a reflection on some other past worlds of university life, and as readers of myths, novels, fantasies and histories know, awareness of other worlds can have an impact on — and change — the real one in which we live.

2

HOW OLD IS THE UNIVERSITY?

I have worked most of my life in Cambridge, at one of what they call the 'old Universities', set in, of course, a beautiful town, with gothic colleges scattered throughout.

On a summer's day it is a pleasure to guide friends and visitors through the colleges, taking in the glories of King's College chapel towering over the green lawns, or cutting through dark and seemingly secret passages to emerge into the medieval court of Corpus Christi, or to see the wisteria-draped walls of Sidney Sussex.

On a wind-swept, cold November afternoon as the darkness falls, it is less enjoyable, but even then, as chapel lights glow through stained glass windows, it remains a place of beauty.

Inquisitive visitors usually want to know all the facts — who founded Queens' College (try to avoid getting bogged down into where the apostrophes go in the various colleges names)? Where did Darwin study? Where Isaac Newton? Where Thandie Newton? Swelling with pride at the antiquity and lustre, frequently aided by a swift check on Google on the phone, one answers — by rival Queens, Margaret of Anjou and Elizabeth

Woodville, Christ's, Trinity and Downing respectively. If in doubt, Henry VIII or Jesus are good all-purpose answers.

People seem to be particularly interested in how old is this college or that one. This is, by and large, easy, as there is usually an answer — Peterhouse, the oldest, was founded in 1284, followed (among the ones that survived, as closing colleges down is not just a twenty-first century thing) by Clare College in 1326, and so on through to Robinson in 1977.

If you wonder how much of a nerd I must be to know this, it's because I'm an evolutionary biologist, and biologists have to come up with analogies for how old life is, as 'three and a half billion' is hard to grasp.

Usually one compares it to 24 hours, when life appears at 4 a.m., life on land around 10 p.m., and humans, pause for drama, only in the last two minutes before the end of the day. Years, hundred-metre races, and, for Bill Bryson, the span of da Vinci's Vitruvian Man, all serve equally well. To add local colour, I used the foundation of the colleges for this purpose, so that Peterhouse was full of single-cell organisms, and Downing dinosaurs. Good for cultivating college rivalry and inverting the normal reputational statuses of the colleges.

Life gets a bit harder if asked 'how old is the University?' The year 1209 is claimed. I have a lapel badge saying that, the only gift I have ever received from the University, so it must be true. However, all that refers to is when some refugee migrants from Oxford moved to Cambridge, an unlikely model for celebration in these times.

In 1226, Cambridge invented its own Charter, and in 1231 King Henry III made it more than self-advertising when he recognised Cambridge as a scholarly institution. The first college was founded in 1284. In practice the whole package was gradually put together over a hundred years, and so you can pretty well pick any date for the founding of the University, and any number for how old.

I pick 10 years, or thereabouts. Admittedly a bit younger than most historians would accept and undoubtedly controversial, so let me explain.

At Department and other committee meetings, there are the usual exciting items on the agenda, as there have always been — student admission numbers and quotas, timetables, use of space, what biscuits for the tea-room. These are discussed, for the most part in the same way — one colleague wants more students, another wants fewer, nobody wants 9 a.m. Monday or Friday afternoon, everyone hasn't got enough space, and the biscuits are impossible to resolve.

But in the last decade or more a new player has crept into these discussions — 'the University'. The Head of Department will suggest that 'the University thinks we should have more students', or 'the University has centralised the timetable' or 'the University has imposed a formula for space allocation'. As far as I know the University has no views on biscuits other than that they must come from a preferred supplier.

It took me a while to realise the seismic shift that was taking place in Cambridge, and I am sure in other universities as well. I had, of course, across my many years as lecturer and professor, talked about the University, often very favourably, but it was never as something separate from me, from my colleagues, from the students.

We were all the University. We, the University, may not have the rhetorical power of 'We the People', but it does represent the idea of the University as it was founded, and as it was over hundreds of years — a community of scholars, a mixture of students and teachers, a home for research groups, and above all, a self-governing institution.

Universities vary in their governance, but at Cambridge at least, it is the Regent House that is sovereign, and that is, broadly speaking, all the academics who provide the research, the money, and attract and teach the students. To refer to the University as anything other than this community would stray a long way from this understood usage.

And yet this is what has happened. To my younger colleagues, 'the University' is 'them'. Indeed, it is probably, in their minds, 'The University', rather than 'the University'. It is a place from which directives and instructions come. It is a place from which permission must be sought, and by which approval is granted. It is the source of power and policy, and as remote from them as the Royal Court to a medieval peasant. It is the 'they' heard so often in British discourse generally.

It would, though, be quite hard to pin down exactly who 'they' are. In my more cynical moments, it is of course Human Resources, as it is in many modern institutions, that are the dark sources of power. At other times it is a more benign amalgam of the various pro-vice-chancellors and deans and heads. More usually it is just 'the administration', or possibly 'The Administration'.

I am sure there is no explicit definition of 'The University', nor even any self-recognition of those most likely to be 'The University'. Maybe even within the depths of a university administration, there are outer echelons who refer to 'The University' as something other, and this continues in ever decreasing circles. Much as I would like to believe there are secret handshakes and mason-like meetings, the sad truth is that the power of 'The University' comes from the fact that it is as much in our heads as in any grand or cunning plan.

How and why did we manage to change from 'We the University' to 'They the University', a move I think has happened in all universities, in some probably to an even greater extent. There is no doubt that the shift was in part due to external pressures. The call for accountability and endless reporting demanded more and more of a central response and central decision-making process.

A former Vice-Chancellor said to me once, when I moaned

about the increasing managerial approach, that the University was statutorily required to provide more than 500 pieces of data to central government each year.

However, much is also self-inflicted, or at least arises from the complicity between external pressures and internal strategies. Most of these revolve around the monetisation of higher education; more and more money is not just the currency of operation, but also the blood that flows through the universities' arteries and veins, and money requires, again, more centralisation. We can't all have our own individual bank accounts in the university!

And it is probably a sad fact of life that where money is involved, the door is slammed on democracy, and the more the money, the faster and tighter the doors close. The result is empowering those at the centre, and disempowering those on the periphery, and ironic as it may seem, it was the lumpen-academics who were at the periphery. These doors we stare at turn out to have 'The University' written on them.

With peripheralisation comes disengagement, and so a growing acquiescence to a 'them' and 'us' world, fuelled by impossible workloads, an increasingly competitive and demanding environment in which publications and grants become the focus, and involvement in the mechanics of the University a distraction — much better to leave it to others, and to get on with the next gel/ode/archive/experiment (delete as appropriate). And so the ratchet of centralisation continues — an intimate dance of repelling actors.

Stress, anxiety, increasingly ignorance of the way The University works, and ultimately subservience to hierarchy completes the process. In the deep past, egalitarian hunter-gatherers gave way to more and more hierarchical structures, and perhaps it was the same, inevitable drivers of competition, levels of work, and complexity that made it happen.

Relationships among people in universities have, in the deeper past, been more communal in structure. You did things because there was a genuine sense of working together, and if the Vice-Chancellor said we should help students more, or take some level of pay restraint, it seemed a reasonable arrangement among peers, rather than between employers and employees, let alone between supplier and customer (aka students).

But once the University is 'The University', this appealing to better nature and collegiality has little force, and even less as the pay gap between the Vice-Chancellor and the rest yawns wider and wider — and, in my view, so much more has been lost rather than gained in that change.

I would not suggest for a moment that before 'The University' there was a utopia of that happy band of scholars; there were many other perils and inequalities, but the 'them' and 'us' that structured an often chaotic academic environment seemed more fluid, with individuals moving between them according to situation much more frequently and easily, and the checks and balances against centralisation more effective. I certainly felt more in control of my working life as an anonymous lecturer thirty years ago than as a senior professor in the last decade.

Can anything be done? Probably not, and perhaps those in the know ('The University'?) are right to think that stronger hierarchies, and a citadel of decision makers, is the way in which modern universities can survive and thrive, and navigate the often hostile oceans of higher education, but I can't help feeling that a worse system has replaced a better one.

My only evidence for this is crumbling morale and the stress I see around me. I would also guess that many of the more centralised processes that were brought in to cope with the COVID emergency are likely to remain in place, enlarging the gap between what someone called Eric Blair called the Inner and Outer University[1].

So, next time I am asked how old Cambridge is, I shall release my inner pedant and ask, do you mean the University, or 'The University'? While the University may have been founded in the mists of time, 'The University' is a more recent and possibly sadder foundation.

3

THE LAST TABOO

In academic life — ideally — there should be few if any taboos. If academic freedom means anything, it is a licence to think out loud.

Sometimes that may of course bring down unhappy consequences on the person doing the thinking out loud, so in practice academic freedom is hemmed in on one side by the sensitivity of the receiver and the courage — or stupidity — of the thinker. As issues to do with race and other aspects of diversity have come to the fore, these fences have perhaps shifted. There is, though, one taboo that a lecturer or professor breaks at their own peril.

Imagine that you go into the staff-room, post-room, lunch, or a colleague's office, and he or she asks you how you are. You reply:

> Absolutely fantastic. I can't wait to charge through my emails — always educational and informative — and then I have a couple of lectures — my favourite subject and such great students — before I look over the latest

> REF submissions (such clever colleagues we have). Pigs in clover fails to catch the perfection of my day.

Wrong! You have just made an error, a cultural gaffe of enormous magnitude. You have broken the ultimate tribal taboo of academia — *do not be uncomplaining about your lot.* In the less benign days of Druids and woad you would have ended up as a set of choice cuts on the altar at Stonehenge. You would now, though, be first in line when volunteers for redundancy are being tracked down.

As every academic reader of this will know, the correct answer to anyone asking how you are is:

> Oh God, you have no idea. My inbox is swamped with illiterate instructions from on high, all wanting a response by yesterday. My eleven o'clock lecture isn't ready, the PowerPoint froze and ate 10 slides, I haven't read the Master's students' coursework, and this afternoon I have to listen to Bloggs droning on about how awful the REF submission is.

Unlike the earlier answer, this one is the perfect prompt for a full and fascinating conversation, and the beginning of that key but largely untutored academic skill — the competitive moan.

> Yes, that does sound bad, but you don't know the half of it. My inbox was so full my email shut down, I haven't a clue what I am supposed to be lecturing about at ten, and there's an endless stream of students waiting to see me. Not to mention my paper has come back with major revisions, and Reviewer 2 is clearly moronic.

Once started, this exchange becomes its own renewable energy source.

Among the indigenous communities of the Pacific coast of

the US and Canada there is a custom known as potlatch. This is a competitive gift-giving feast, where the winner is the one who gives the most away — even at the cost of complete penury. In the Ivory Flats, we have competitive moaning. The winner is the person who has the most to complain about. Actually, that is not quite true. The winner is person who complains best.

This will occasionally reflect genuine hardship, overwork and deprivation, but to be honest, there is a skill in the game that only bears a loose relationship to the pecking order of suffering. Some people are just good at it. Indeed, as we get trained for everything else these days, we should probably have courses devoted to it.

There are two puzzles about this local cultural tradition. One is that I am not sure when it began. I don't recall it being a big thing in the 1970s when I started lecturing, just the odd minor moan, although no doubt there were early specialists.

I did have one colleague who could sigh for England. His timing was perfect — if somebody entered the departmental office, he could ensure that his soft, long, low sigh was not drowned by the door closing. If you walked past his office, the sigh came exactly as you passed the open door. Many a neophyte made the mistake of stopping and asking what was wrong.

But he was an outlier, an evolutionarily precocial mammal-like reptile lurking in the Palaeozoic. For the most part we seemed as cheerful as could be expected.

More precisely, moans were specific, targeted, not generic. A particular lecture, not the whole livelihood of teaching; a particular student, not the entire student body in this and any other university, at this time or any other time, a singularly unhelpful reviewer, not the entire peer review system.

It is hard to pinpoint when the transition took place, and it is probably not so much a point in time as a response to the changing conditions in which we work — as we moved out of the Ivory Tower and into the Ivory Flats. If I was to pick on one thing, it would be the growth of email, removing the camouflage that allowed us to shelter safely from institutional predators, and get on with our work, but it is difficult to disentangle this from the relentless growth of a central administration with few inhibitions and less accountability.

The other puzzle is why this has become the central cultural tradition, as much a part of being an academic as speaking French is to being French. That it is so pervasive is probably easily understandable, an outcome of the normal processes of cultural evolution. In learning the skills of the culture, to do well and rise up, one is well-advised to imitate the behaviours that are most common, or failing that, the behaviours of those with the highest status.

Either way, once moaning becomes common, only a fool will not moan. To use one of my favourite evolutionary models, John Maynard Smith's 'evolutionarily stable strategy', it is uninvadable by a strategy with a higher payoff. In a universe of complainers, the happy rat is a loser.

More difficult to understand than the spread is the origin. It is unlikely to be the result of one particularly charismatic complainer, the 'moaner zero' in modern pandemic terminology. More probable is that the conditions in which we work have changed.

I have already referred to emails, usually at the top of most people's list of curses of modern academic life. Emails destroy planning. They are the great disruptor. No matter what one sets out to do, only the most focused of us (not me) is not side-tracked by the ping, and so the day unravels like a badly knitted jumper. But emails — there is so much more to say on those — are not unique to universities, so cannot be more than the collateral damager.

Another possible culprit is the sheer increase in workload. What better reason is there to complain than that we are working too hard, too many hours. That is certainly true — I look back at my younger years as if they were leisurely Edwardian summers, compared to the frantic pace today.

But while academics work hard and long hours — most do more than 50 hours a week, and Mary Beard recently said she worked 100 hours — young bankers and city folk are regularly doing 120 or more (mind you, their burn-out rate is phenomenal), and they probably complain less, either because they are too busy counting the money, or because it would be seen as a sign of weakness, not being able to cut it in the fat-cat race.

I think we have to look at the tensions that lie within academic life these days. Those tensions are what makes us unable either to rise up in full-blown strikes and revolt, nor happily accept our lot. Moaning is the resolution to those tensions.

Two ways in which we are pulled in different directions come to mind. The first is teaching and research. I think, back in the days when we lived in Ivory Towers, there was a general acceptance that teaching, lecturing, was a central part of the role, rewarding in itself, and not that overwhelming.

Research was equally important, and usually why people entered the career. However, everyone found their own balance, with some enjoying and focusing more on teaching, others research, and the balance could shift back and forth across a career.

There has, though, been a change in this balance. Leaving aside that teaching has become time-consuming (finding the perfect picture of a baby gorilla for one PowerPoint can take hours!), the relative status of the two has changed. The REF, and universities' obsession with grant income, has elevated research as 'the activity', the basis for respect, reputation and promotion. This may have been inevitable, and indeed what most of us who are 'research active' would like, but the unintended consequence is the resentment of time spent teaching. Lecturing, tutoring, and student support become, in our heads, the things that are keeping us from that Nobel Prize.

Given the increasing amount of work time now devoted to all

of these, and the way in which research becomes squeezed into the margins of the working day and year, what was previously a more balanced situation has become a major stressor. Moaning —'I have another ten lectures this week and that grant deadline is approaching faster than a speeding bullet' — is the only solution, as, in practice, not much else can be done.

We work in this extraordinary environment where the only thing that counts — research — is not scheduled. Imagine being a surgeon where no theatre time is scheduled, just meetings and training. Finding time to make a few incisions would just have to be squeezed into evenings and weekends. That is modern university life.

The second tension lies in the ambiguity of academic employment. In Flann O'Brien's *The Third Policeman*, the people of the village spend so long riding their bicycles that they exchange molecules with them, so that the bicycle takes on human characteristics, and the humans bike ones. A person can have a slow puncture, and a bike can have a personality.

Working in a university for a long time also results in an exchange of molecules, so that where you stop and the institution starts becomes horrendously blurred. We are not really simple employees earning a wage, as we are so invested in our institutions, and our lives and egos are locked into those institutions.

At the sadder end there are those, despite the complete change in the nature of our relationship with our employers, who have stayed in love with the process of research and teaching. To change would be accepting the end of the affair. The solution, of course, is to moan.

> It's ridiculous, they've put me on the Working After Hours Safety Committee, but what can I do... That's another late-nighter I shall have finishing my grant application.

So moaning is the adaptive solution, the academic safety

valve, where we cannot rise up and revolt against our lot, because we think it would be revolting against ourselves, hurting our colleagues and friends and students. The growing distinction between 'The University' and the academics erodes that sense of community, and perhaps ultimately moaning will be replaced by a different adaptive solution. Until then, it is much easier just to ratchet up the potlatch of complaints. '*I'll see your 50 hours of lectures and three committees and raise you...*'

Moaning is, paradoxically, the offspring of impotence.

4

WHY WE ARE ALL FOLDING NAPKINS NOW

Imagine there are two activities going on in your Department: buttering toast and folding napkins.

Buttering toast is, in everyone's reckoning, more important than folding napkins. Buttered toast is tasty, essential for thinking and productivity, can be mixed with lots of other things according to need and taste (jam, honey, marmite), and the Department has attracted some very talented toast-butterers, and indeed has a strong international reputation for the toast-butter interface. And besides, you can always wipe your fingers and mouth on your sleeve.

However, for reasons lost in the bowels of some email, folding napkins has to be organised at a higher level, as all napkins have to be folded the same way, whereas buttering toast can be left to the butterer.

So, a Director of Napkin Folding is appointed in the central administration, soon to be followed by a couple of NF support staff, as it turns out to be quite complex to coordinate across the University, where previously triangles, rectangles, squares and those funny swan-like things, have flourished. Soon directives and forms are flying around, as harmonisation of napkin folding continues apace.

People have less and less time to butter the toast, as they are filling in napkin forms and learning the 'preferred', and then 'approved', way of folding. The Department's reputation for Toast Buttering Science, begins to fall and it gets squeezed into shorter and shorter periods of time. Inevitably, this is put down to the greater success and importance of napkin folding, so a few more NF staff are appointed. Even though fewer napkins are needed as no one is making toast anymore, they continue to multiply.

And, as you may be wondering where this is going, this is the payoff. Any central assessment of activity in the Department can now see that Napkin Folding is more important than toast-buttering, and indeed toast-buttering is entirely dependent upon napkin folding. Everybody is now feverishly creating piles of folded napkins.

This in turn can be ascribed to the effectiveness of the central administration's Napkin Folding Division (promotions all round!), and so also to the success of centralising. In contrast, it could be said that toast-buttering failed because it lacked central leadership, coordination and proper management. Eventually, the end comes when only a few dried crumbs are left on a table heaving with napkins.

Alright, an exaggeration perhaps, but this is a process we have all seen happening, although you might want to replace buttering toast and napkin folding with something more appropriate like research or teaching on the one hand instead of toast-buttering, and management instead of napkin folding on the other, perhaps.

Ask virtually any academic about how they spend their time, and there will be time spent teaching, time spent doing research, but more and more there is time spent on activities that can best be described as supportive, ancillary or peripheral to research and teaching (which of those three words — supportive, ancillary or peripheral — you prefer is likely to vary depending on where you lie in the university ecosystem). Strategic committees on research, teaching planning, student feedback, curriculum reviews, REF planning, REF post-mortems, pre-grant application assessments by various levels within the university, risk assessments, and many, many reports are where the time increasingly goes.

Napkin folding is not entirely irrelevant to buttering toast, but it is not the objective itself, and the same is true of the core activities — research and teaching — and the ancillary activities. Ultimately one could eat buttered toast without a napkin, although it is better to have one, but how carefully and uniformly folded it is may not matter that much.

And here we come to the heart of what I want to say. I am not someone who believes there is a conspiracy to make lives harder for the lumpen-academic, or indeed much other than good intentions among the 'powers that be', but I am interested in the processes by which 'things just happen that way'. In this case, it relates to the consequences of what I would call 'centralisability', an ugly but essential word.

Some tasks either have to be more centralised, or more importantly, *can* be centralised, others cannot, or cannot without changing them irrevocably. Centralisability is a measure of how easy it is to centralise something. It is scale free — collaborators on a paper require some centralisation, university finance departments a lot. However, the centralisability of a task should not be an indication of, or proxy for, its importance to the institution, and in many cases it is exactly the reverse.

Indeed, it may even be the case that there is a law, like Murphy's Law, that the easier it is to centralise something, the less important it is to the actual life of the institution.

This would make some sort of sense, as to a large extent the more centralisable something is, the less specific, and so the less it connects to local mentalities and contexts, and the greater the potential for distancing, for a sense of peripheralization. It is this that I mean by the 'processes by which things just happen', and, of course, have happened.

Once activities have come, for better or for worse, under more central management, they will inevitably become more important to the institution than those that have not. This is partly because they are more visible to the central powers, as the activity is closer to them, and so flows more fully and easily through the institution's bloodstream, and partly because there is now a greater administrative investment. The more the investment, the more important the activity.

That is how — remember where we started — that what was generally accepted as the most important (and enjoyable!) activity, buttering toast, came to be replaced by the less important (and less enjoyable) one of folding napkins.

It would probably not have been intentional (except perhaps to the occasional napkin folding fanatic), but is an almost inevitable consequence of centralisation in a system that, by and large, has thrived and flourished on local independence — Cambridge (and Oxford) perhaps being prime examples.

These thoughts have been prompted by watching my university transform itself from a dynamic and distributed network of toast-butterers, into a less happy and less successful (although that's a bit of a napkin-folding assessment based on league tables) body of napkin folders. They were perhaps crystalised by a friend sending me an old article from 2012 by Kurt Eichewald in *Vanity Fair*, on the decline of Microsoft. Towards the end there is a comment from Steve Jobs[1] on the failure years of Apple.

> The company starts valuing the great salesmen, because they're the ones who can move the needle on revenues, not the product engineers and designers. So the salespeople end up running the company... [Then] the product guys don't matter so much, and a lot of them just turn off.

In universities it is not the salespeople, but (and this is shared with salespeople) those most visible to the centre, the ones immediately seen to be having an effect on whatever needle is being watched, who become valued, and more peripheral people, even if they are the actual drivers of the institution's success, become increasingly invisible. That sense of being invisible to the people at the top of the university did not seem to exist so much when I started, but now I think is an implicit perception amongst many. And being invisible tends to lower morale unless you happen to be in a superhero film.

I do not have easy solutions, but recognising the problem is a starting point. One possible improvement might be to stop the drift towards seeing the activities of academics falling into three different realms — teaching, research and administration. This implies an equivalence, but is in fact a categorical confusion between ends and means. Teaching and research are our core activities, and anything else we do — as indeed we must — should clearly be seen as a means to those ends. Toast buttering is the end (or even eating the toast), and the napkins a way of minimising the resulting mess, but they are not an end in themselves.

Perhaps napkin folding is our inevitable destiny, but I hope people still at least eat buttered toast on occasion.

5

IN PRAISE OF EPHEMERALITY

In 1998, the film *The Truman Show* was released to both financial and critical success. Starring Jim Carey, it told the story of a man who from birth was brought up on a film set, and whose life was broadcast continuously, from infancy to adulthood and marriage.

His whole environment was made up of actors, and his life plotted out daily by the scriptwriters. The film inspired endless debates about reality, religion and the power of television. More than twenty year later, though, there is more than an echo of *The Truman Show* in the everyday life of academics.

The main theme of *The Truman Show* was that the eponymous Truman lived a scripted and controlled life, in an entirely different world from those outside the filmset reality. Even more striking was that it was entirely public, although of course he was unaware of this.

But there is another aspect, which in the days of streaming and box sets, has become more pertinent — its permanence. In the fictional world outside the Truman set (so not the real real world, but the fictional real world) people could in principle replay particular bits of Truman's life at any time, pause it, dissect it, and check what he said or did at any moment of time. In other words, it was not just the artificiality and public nature of his life, but the fact that it was there to be recalled and rewatched forever.

Unlikely as it may seem, university life is converging on the Truman Story.

How so? Even before COVID-19, there was a move towards the recording of events. I gave a seminar in Oxford in 2018, and it was the tradition of the organisers to stream this. Now common practice, this was the first time this applied to one of my talks. I gave another lecture recently, and that was put up on my Department's YouTube channel. About the same time I started giving lectures that were recorded and uploaded, for students to watch in their own time. Streaming and recording of seminars was becoming more and more frequent prior to COVID-19, and since then has continued apace.

Streaming, recording and uploading to the cloud reflected a growing openness of scientific and scholarly communication, and often more than a nod towards equality of access to information. YouTube channels and websites full of TED-ish talks are also, no doubt, useful pieces of institutional and personal advertising.

Recording may also have been a trend influenced by the development of MOOCs, although there is a vast gap between the professionalism of most MOOCs, pioneered of course by the Open University, and the dimly lit home-made movies of most recordings.

COVID-19 took this to an almost Himalayan level. In my department many lectures are pre-recorded, and uploaded, either as a batch *à la* Netflix, or titillatingly embargoed week by week, hopefully with each lecture ending on a cliff-hanger. ...'Watch next week to find out what happens when another factorial is added'... Even lectures given live are recorded, helpful both to those for whom once is never enough and for those unable to attend.

And not just lectures. Then there are meetings that are

recorded, to make minutes easier, and often put on intranets, so that sending your apologies that you sadly can't attend the timetabling sub-committee is no longer the get out of jail free card that it once was.

This is getting close to *The Truman Show* territory — in a busy week your average lecturer might crank up to twenty hours of their lives permanently on record. When I was a child my parents would take me to their friends' houses, and after dinner there would often be the 'let's get out the slides of our summer holiday camping in the Brecon Beacons', a prelude to hours of boredom, often upside-down boredom. Future academic parties might become similar occasions of terror:

> After dinner, would you like to watch a few clips from my withering put downs of Professor Jones at the last departmental meeting, and I also have some interesting footage of my thoughts on the biology of the liver fluke.

Perhaps more seriously, there is the fear of loss of privacy, for who knows in what institutional bowels these things may be stored for a later date:

> Dr Loostung, you may be interested to know that Professor Jones has just been appointed Pro-Vice-Chancellor for Human Resources, and he thought you might like to listen to these recordings...

Many lecturers have also looked suspiciously at the release agreements that have to be signed, with suitably ambiguous phrases about the university having the right to do pretty much what they like with the recordings:

> While we are obviously sad to hear that Professor Eggspert is retiring, some consolation can be taken from the fact that he has been replaced, at much lower cost, by

> an external disk drive, and his lectures will be no more out of date than they usually are. I am glad to say we are working on algorithms that will allow him to still make his valuable interventions at meetings, but at twice the speed.

The issues of privacy and rights are serious, but they are also tangible enough for regulations and laws to hold the worst potential excesses in check. It is the intangible loss of ephemerality that concerns me. While some teaching and research talks involve a written script, in the sciences at least, a lecture or seminar is 'a talk'.

It's my experience, certainly in recent years, these are largely done without notes at all. PowerPoint has made this much easier, although the temptation to put the entire script on the slides is often too much for some. But most of us 'talk to the slides', which are helpful prompts. Speaking for myself, what they prompt is not necessarily always the same thing! I might look at a graph and be inspired by one element of it on one occasion, and a different one on another.

Qualifications about results may on occasion be skipped due to lack of time. Claims that go beyond the data might be helpfully provocative, but can also be hostages to fortune. Sometimes an entirely new thought will come to me, and it is something one shares instinctively and with the hope of useful questions and suggestions.

Sadly, that entirely new thought might turn out to be an entirely wrong thought, but now would be preserved if not for ever, certainly for long enough to cause embarrassment.

And then there are the jokes and the offhand remarks. Admittedly these can be scripted. A social anthropology colleague of mine was asked by his very distinguished professor to give his lecture at the last minute. He was handed a set of scruffy pages. These were the complete text, so it was just a matter of reading the lecture. All went well until he turned the page, where a break in the text was marked in handwriting — 'Tell the Inuit joke here'. Which, of course, he didn't know.

But sometimes witticisms just arrive in the head, and out they tumble. Usually they are local, often personal, and may relate to who is in the audience. There may be a bit of chit-chat, corrections from the audience, and even heckling. These are things of the moment, seldom good enough to be preserved for posterity. They are deeply contextual, and prone to the swirling changes of intellectual fashion. Not to mention changing generations.

I came to realise sometime ago that clever allusions to dead parrots referred to television events more than fifty years ago, before the parents of the current crop of students were born, let alone the students themselves! But ad libs and improvised segments were alright, as the thought, the joke, even the bright insight, would fade after the talk with the certainty of a short isotopic half-life, and the decay could be accelerated by a nice post-seminar visit to the pub.

But this has now changed, perhaps forever. A recorded, uploaded, clouded seminar is forever. The ephemeral has become digitally engraved.

Tweeters (Xers?) and Facebook users have discovered this, often to their cost. Juvenile rashness and unguarded comments have brought a number of careers to an abrupt end. It is unlikely that many of our online lectures will be sufficiently interesting for that to happen, but there is the matter of context. The visiting seminar in Oxford is likely to be seen in an entirely different light in Delhi or Delaware.

The effect on the speaker might be global embarrassment, but it is more likely that caution and sensitivity will lead to overwhelming blandness. For disciplines where discovery is competitive it has already led to talks being restricted to what has already been published, and novel ideas are seldom presented.

In the search for generality in trying to understand these consequences, I am drawn to comparisons with globalisation. There are many benefits to globalisation, not least the greater networking across different part of the world, and the same is true of our ability to share ideas, discoveries, methods much more widely.

But as with globalisation, there are costs as well, and the primary one is the loss of the local. While I do not want to overdo a comparison between my seminars and a wonderful artisan French cheese, both benefit from being local, having a local context, what the French call *terroir*; they involve experiences that occur in a particular time and place.

Streaming and global lectures and seminars run the risk of replacing Reblochon with Babybel. Not to mention, of course, that where we all used to trot around the country with the same talk, we now have to come up with something new every time, as there is a good chance that it is the same audience!

So, a small tear for lost ephemerality, for the weakening of the local, and for the blandness of context-free academia, and the risk of corny jokes growing even staler.

With search engines, all is lost. Or rather, not lost.

6

FORGET THE TIME MANAGEMENT COURSES, ASK THE PEAHEN

Lewis Carroll wrote or received, across most of his adult life, more than 98,000 letters.

That would seem to be an impressively large number. Carroll recorded, in a series of index books, all the letters he wrote and received, with details of dates, writer, topic.

I do not have his patience, so I put all non-spam emails, sent and received, in a folder optimistically called 'All Done'. At the end of the year, I put a date on it, and start another one. Looking over my annual 'All Done' folders for the last decade, they are never less than 20,000 per year. In five years, I can amass a lifetime of Carroll's correspondence.

His are probably witty and informative; sadly most of mine are either reminders of things I have to do or have neglected to do, as well as fascinating information about the latest course on how to manage my time. The comprehensive edition of my forthcoming twenty-volume collected emails will be riveting, at least in the sense that it will fix for once and for all the mind-numbing way we spend the days in our Ivory Flats.

Twenty thousand a year amounts to more than 50 per day (and that excludes Nigerian princes and invitations to guest edit the journal of integrated gynaecological engineering), and involves a substantial quantity of time spent daily in reading, responding, procrastinating, and it doesn't really matter whether you are one of those people who assiduously empties the inbox as fast as it fills, or, more moth-like, are drawn irresistibly to the brightness of new or unanswered emails, only to shy away from them time and time again.

Emails are a time-sump. The average professional, and academics probably still qualify, spends 28% of their working day on emails.[1] That adds up to more than a quarter of our working year. Put another way, more than a quarter of the University's salary budget is devoted to emailing! We can probably now add social media to the average time budget. Even without including time spent looking at political polemics and funny memes, Twitter (now X) is an endlessly renewed source of academic information, and as inboxes have flooded, WhatsApp has become a work overflow drainage system.

I am hardly the first to complain about the way in which email has transformed, and largely worsened, our working lives — the number, the banality, the tedium of 'kindly reminders', the hijacking of our own priorities, the perpetual guilt, the Sisyphean nature of the task, and the flattening of all relationships into a two-dimensional list. And I certainly won't be the last.

I do, though, have a modest proposal to improve our lives. It involves two things that are seldom brought together — the Royal Mail and evolutionary theory.

The first postage stamp was issued in Britain in 1840, and is recognised as a revolution in communication. This revolution might appear to be one of just finding an efficient system of payment, but it is deeper than that.

As far as I know, before stamps, the cost of sending post

was largely paid for by the recipient, not the sender. You put the letter in the post, and the person it was addressed to would be asked for payment. They could, of course, simply refuse to accept it. (A bill? Victorian junk mail? Imagine the temptation.) Economically it makes much more sense to charge the sender, as payment is guaranteed and upfront. The post office learnt early the importance of putting the cost on the sender.

Who pays, sender or receiver, is actually a serious question. Not just for postal services, but across the whole biological world. We think of evolution as being about fitting in with the environment, who has the better camouflage, who is effective at finding food, and so on, but for all species, plants animals, fungi, the lot, it is about sending signals — signals to mates, saying I am fitter (larger horns), signals to mates saying I am fertile (genital tumescence), signals to predators (I am poisonous), signals to competitors (I am bigger than you), signals to pollinators (look at my pretty colours). The firefly is not just flashing for fun.

The continuity of life is dependent upon successful signalling. And this turns out to be a bit of a tug of war between the signaller and the receiver. The signaller wants to persuade the receiver of something — their status perhaps — and do this as cheaply as possible. You want to be big — have a big shaggy coat that inflates your size. You want to look healthy — have bright shiny feathers that hide your parasite-ridden body.

The receiver, on the other hand, wants to be sure the signal is honest, not some cheap advertising trick. From the receiver's point of view, better for the signal to be a long, risky, time-consuming ritual of courtship to test the quality of the mate, than to be a smile and a wink.

The peacock's tail is a classic example — an encumbrance to movement, an energetic expense to grow and maintain, rather visible to predators, but worth its weight in feathers reproductively speaking. The peahen knows it's honest because the peacock is paying a high cost. In the co-evolution of signalling, natural selection has favoured the honest signaller (except for those crafty mimicking insects) over the trickster, and it is the distribution of costs between the sender and receiver that is key.

The result of this tussle across the biosphere is that honest signals are costly to the sender, dishonest signals cheap. 'Receiver beware of bargain messages' is the lesson of evolution. It is also a lesson for us in a world saturated by emails.

Virtually everyone in a working environment deplores the corrosive effect of email on our lives, both before and during the pandemic. The costs to a university or company's time and productivity are well-known, as is the stress to individuals. Imposed and voluntary restrictions are appearing — for example having 'no email' days. We all now receive emails with tags saying emails are only checked in working hours (please define).

However, this is applying a band-aid to an artery cut — the emails would still keep coming, and the onus would remain on the receiver to ignore the flow.

What would be more effective would be to learn from biology, or, indeed, the Royal Mail. Sending emails is not just cheap, but effectively free to the writer. All the costs lie with the receiver. A one-line email from an administrator to thirty people might take them a minute, but it is likely that each receiver will spend considerably more reading, thinking, responding, deleting!

Multiple receivers multiply the costs to all but the sender. It can be innocuous — a keen student might send the same email to all the professors of evolution in the UK with an interesting question (it happens), soaking up hours of time across the university sector. It can be innocent but unwittingly time-consuming.

An email sent a few years ago to a very large number of Cambridge academics asked them to fill in an Excel spreadsheet with all their international contacts, with details — a few minutes for the sender, a summed cost for all recipients of probably hundreds of hours.

It can, of course, also be malicious — a scam to millions of people, effectively free to the scammer, probably takes a few seconds for most to read and delete — but that is hours and hours of time across a year for receivers, and, for a few, major losses to a dishonest signaller. This is not to say there are no costs for the sender — who has not pressed the send button only to regret it instantly?

Email is a complete pain, wrecks personal work priorities, enforces power relationships, and invades the home. It also goes against the wisdom of millions of years of evolution. Sending is cheap (and therefore open to dishonesty), and the recipient pays the bill in time, risk, stress and even money. To stem the flow, the costs need to be returned to the sender.

There are a number of ways that can be done, probably at all levels. It has always astounded me that Chancellors of the Exchequer haven't eyed up emails for a microtax. In 2021, there were 319.6 billion emails sent per day worldwide. If every email cost even a small amount to send (payable to a government green fund?), it could raise an enormous amount of revenue, spam will dry up, and mailing lists pruned (taxed per numbers of recipients, not number sent, of course).

But there are more local solutions as well. We used to have the Department postal budget, which involved writing your initials on the corner of envelopes and running to catch the last post. It was all fairly miserable, and email has to be an improvement on departmental secretarial disapproval of my letter-writing behaviour, but it did put the costs on the sender. Not all these costs were entirely monetary: *'Are you sure this is Departmental business, Dr Foley, as it is clearly addressed to your mother, and why is this one first class... is it really urgent?'*

But the digital world has always allowed greater precision in allocating costs. When I first started using computers as a student at Cambridge in the early 1970s, PCs did not exist, and we would troop into the computer centre to load our programmes into the card reader late at night (you haven't lived until you have spent time in a computer room at 11 p.m.).

You would then wait until the next day to collect the printout. This was often depressingly thin, if there had been a bug in the programme. When this happened, it meant waiting another day and night to rerun it.

The reason was that all users had a share in the system, entitling you to so much resource per week. As a student, this was only a small amount, and needed to be hoarded carefully. One way was to schedule programmes to run overnight, with lower costs. Only when you were really excited and impatient — or frustrated — would you splurge on a daytime run.

This would work perfectly today with email. We would all have a digital budget, and we could spend it as we wished — a witty joke to a hundred colleagues, or a hundred emails to one collaborator discussing the eleventh dimension or the immateriality of (either) Madonna. Resources could reflect the number of students taught, the number of books published, perhaps there might even be an H-index bonus. Rules would have to be in place to ensure most resources went to academics, of course, otherwise...

There could also be different costs depending on whether the email goes at set times (welcome back, the morning and afternoon post), or immediately (remember telegrams?).

Email is a boon to many, allowing swift and easy communication, and enhancing access to and for many people. However, against the grain of communication systems in nature, the recipients are paying the costs, and in many cases these have risen to intolerable levels.

It is this imbalance in costs (and benefits) that has allowed email to spiral out of control. We would all think twice if each email cost a digital Penny Black. We should learn from the peahen, make the sender pay, and reclaim our time.

7

WHEN ACTIONS SPEAK LOUDER THAN ORGANOGRAMS

There is an old joke that vets are better than doctors because they can't ask their patients what is wrong. They have to base their diagnosis on the behaviour of the patient, rather than self-reporting.

Of course, the dog about to lose its evolutionary potential, may have different views on the costs and benefits of being able to self-report. I have no idea whether this belief is true or not. However, the difference — alleged — between doctors and vets can be surprisingly insightful about university administration.

Until about ten or so years ago — perhaps more, as age is a known telescoper of the past — when I went to work I would pass the departmental office, and usually exchange a few words with the secretaries there.

Over the course of the day, I would probably meet and talk to all the support staff — administrators, technicians, computer officers, custodians — several times. This had a number of effects — communication was fast and nuanced (a raised eyebrow was enough to know my advice was superfluous, so much better than a passive aggressive email); it was a two-way process, implicitly transactional (I'll check those figures if you will return all those graduate applications you're sitting on — unsaid, of course); and merged naturally with gossip, admiration of photos of dogs and children, and a moan about whoever happened to be the villain of the day.

Now, both during and since the pandemic, one sees fewer people, if any. One's administrative colleagues have become a chequerboard of faces on a screen at best, and at worst a name on an email. But even before that, things had changed. Secretaries were rebranded as administrators, and one of the differences between secretaries and administrators is that while the former have their doors open, the latter have them shut.

The other is that where secretaries owed any loyalty they might have to their department or division, administrators owe theirs further up the ladder, centrally, not locally. This coincided with most universities deciding that localism was outmoded. With email there was, it was argued, no longer a need for secretaries or administrators to be in the same building as the academics, and that way there could be greater efficiency.

Cambridge now has a Unified Administrative Service (the clue is in the name), and at its start a senior administrator said that it didn't matter where a job was done, as long as it was done. This had echoes of globalisation, where it also didn't matter where things were done, as long as they were done in the most cost-effective way. That largely meant that the money was in the centre and the labour at the peripheries. With this greater centralisation there was no need for generalists, but instead specialist roles that could be applied across several departments or units. Out went the foxes, and in came the hedgehogs.[1] So no longer the daily chat and update on the daughter's ballet lessons, and instead the digital 'gentle reminder' that you had forgotten to return the risk assessment on opening stationery packages.

What, you are rightly asking, has this to do with doctors and vets? The somewhat tangential link is that there are two ways of finding out how something is working (or not working). One is the doctor's approach — to ask. This is the basis for much work in anthropology. You are interested in marriage patterns, so you go to whomever you are studying, and you ask them who they are allowed to marry. They give you a list of possible partners and a list of prohibited ones. You then have an understanding of how the society works in terms of marriage practices, and certainly a clear perspective on the ideals and perceptions involved.

The second way is the vet's — to watch and observe. Anthropologically that means you find out who is actually married to whom, you go through the marriage register, you go to the ceremonies, you ask no one, but simply watch what actually happens.

You will not be surprised to know that there is not always a match between the two. It is the same with doctors, I am sure. What the patient says is the matter is not necessarily what is. My wife, who is an anthropologist, carried out a nutritional survey in the Amazon many years ago. Part of that was to ask people what they had eaten that day — steak, they would reply. And yesterday? Steak. And the day before? Steak. But she was staying with them, and eating with them, measuring their meals — meals of rice and fish. Today. And yesterday. And the day before.

It is the same with universities. We can ask how it works, and admire the organograms, look at the charts of workflows, read the newsletters and announcements of restructuring, or we can observe. On paper it looks as if nothing has changed in terms of provision of support, or even note it is much better. But if we don't read the emails (such a temptation!), and instead be a vet (or a behavioural ecologist) and just observe and see what actually happens, there is a complete change. No longer are there day to day personal interactions, but occasional encounters to discuss particular things. As with Amazonians, on paper it may say steak every day, but fish and rice it is. Location, location, location, it turns out, is not just about buying houses.

I was prompted to think about this change in behaviour by an article in the *Times Higher Education.*[1] It made two points, and I will give you the good news and the bad news. The good news is that despite a folk view to the contrary, there has not been an increase in the number of administrators in universities. The bad news is that there has been a major increase in the cost of them. The reason for this apparent discrepancy is, of course, that they get paid more, but this is not just HR giving themselves more money.

What has happened is that there has been a change from relatively low-level support staff to higher level managers and senior administrators. And naturally, they are paid more. As John Ross, who wrote the article, says, the level of administrative staff has remained at only 55% (I know, that is still more than half), but what has changed is the proportion — support staff went from about 50% of the administrative staff to less than 15%. Professional staff — those with their own offices and closed doors — are now 60% of general staff.

So my change in behaviour — no more finding out about the secretaries' book club and complaining that Arsenal lost again — is not that I was getting more remote, but that there are only one and a half people to talk to where before there were five! Doctors and anthropologists might be misled by this, but vets would not. What the dog does is what the dog is, and what the dog feels.

Of course, none of this may matter, except to the budget, if the job gets done. Indeed, if the job gets done better, it is money well spent. No doubt some of it does. As Gwilym Croucher, of the Melbourne Centre for the Study of Higher Education, who carried out the research on which this is all based, is reported to have said: 'It requires people to manage those processes and work with governments, and it cultivates an internal culture of compliance checking.'

And we know no greater ambition an academic doth have than 'greater compliance'.

There is no doubt the external pressure on universities for compliance is enormous, and it would be near impossible for an institution simply to ignore the pressures that come not only from government but also from student and public opinion. Some may even be beneficial. That pressure, along with the search for more and more funding, has almost certainly led to the explosion of managerial and senior administrative posts.

That should not necessarily mean there had to be a reduction in actual support for the academics who produce the teaching and research, but something had to go, and it turned out what had to go were the support staff who did the supporting.

And it is the loss of support and its replacement by management that resolves the difference in perception and experience. We have become lazy in complaining about administrators, who are doing the job they have been brought in to do, and conflated that with the issue of loss of support staff who work directly with academics carrying out their job.

Both perspectives are true. The powers that be can point to the extra investment in support and say, what is the problem? And the academics at the chalkface can also say that the support that actually makes a difference to their work — as opposed to the efficiency and well-being of The University — has virtually disappeared, so that they are now doing more and more 'admin' — i.e. the basic support work previously done by the aptly called support staff.

The lesson is that support for the 'The University' and support for academics is not necessarily the same thing, and may even be diametrically opposed. When the trains in Britain ground to a halt many years ago, the company said the problem was that it was the wrong type of leaves on the rails. Academics may also be grinding to a halt because now they have the wrong sort of support.

Perhaps it is not just a case of less support, or the wrong sort of support, but the replacement of support by a system. Distant administration can only deal with the core of the work, and that means systems rules, procedures, guidelines, and forms.

But where on a form can one fill in a comment on the weather? I suppose there could be a tick-box — How are your parents? Well. Been better. Sadly died (go to section 8). These small bits of chit-chat are the lubricants of social interactions, and social interactions are the vehicles by which we work. Systems make the error of assuming that the core is all that matters. It is as if biologists, having recognised that the nucleus is the core of the cell, so discarded the rest — and with it, all the busy little mitochondria that do the work, all the channels of communication between cells, leaving only some highly sprung coils of DNA with their repetitive letters.

And it is not just that the social interactions add a sense of cooperating and so cooperative goals — they do, of course — but also that *ad hoc* face-to-face exchanges with the people we work with are open-ended. What might start as a discussion about the timetable can morph into one about a particular student problem, or the difficulties a colleague may have teaching at a particular time, or indeed, with colleagues this can be the basis for new collaborative ventures.

Now, this all may be completely wrong, because I have withheld a vital fact from the article in the *Times Higher* that triggered these thoughts — the survey was of Australian universities. Perhaps UK ones have retained much tried and trusted administrative principles (Drop In, Have A Chat, and Get it Done), but I rather doubt it. And perhaps worse. At Cambridge since 2010 technical assistant staff increased by 4%, academic staff by 8%, research staff by 43% and academic-related and assistant staff by 49%.[1]

8

GOSH, IS THAT THE TIME?

If I want to shock my younger colleagues, I tell them about my early years as a lecturer.

My first teaching appointment was in 1977, at the University of Durham. It was something nowadays unheard of — a nearly finished PhD, a single scrappy publication, and all of 24 years old. Times were so different then, and I have more than a pang of guilt when I see the current generation wobbling from postdoc to postdoc, clutching armfuls of publications in top journals, glittering with awards and veteran teachers, struggling to find a permanent post.

That's shocking enough, and indeed I can't help but wonder whether I would have survived beyond my PhD in these more competitive times. But to send them into an apoplexy of incredulity I talk about cricket.

Assuming I don't have to explain how cricket works, I tell them how, in my early years as a lecturer I would play cricket for the University Staff team two or three times a week through the summer — from around 4 p.m. on Tuesdays and Thursdays, usually being beaten by the students, and all day on Saturdays for a local club, travelling round the increasingly silent mining villages of Durham.

How on earth, they would ask, did you have the time for this? And indeed, it is a perplexing question even for me. My last ten or fifteen years of teaching and researching at Cambridge before I retired in 2020 were, by comparison, manic. Days filled with meetings, inboxes filled with gentle reminders, lunchtimes filled with seminars, even the occasional lecture and supervision. Weeks would pass in a blur, terms become blank memories of sameness. Where on earth did the time go?

An optimist might say that I was teaching more, giving more time to the students and less to improving my cover drive. This is almost certainly not true, for my lecturing load was higher in Durham than it ever was in Cambridge, and indeed in Cambridge — which I moved to in 1986 — I gave more lectures in the last part of the twentieth century than I did in this one.

Supervising has also declined. For many years I would teach first year students across many colleges, and all the second- and third-year students who took my courses, something that would be unheard of now among my colleagues. In line with the rest of the University, the onus of teaching has moved to the great untenured. So, it's not the teaching.

Perhaps it is my red-hot devotion to research. Certainly, if I look back to those early days, my approach to research was, how shall I put it? — ...more relaxed.

Writing books was still an acceptable form of research, so I was doing that. This involved a lot of reading and thinking (poor batting form at cricket was good for the latter), and was relatively cheap. I needed grants for fieldwork, but these were modest and intended to get me places rather than decorate my CV and boost the University's income.

At the time there also seemed to be a much closer relationship between teaching and research — lectures were almost an integral part of the research process, and it is my impression that a more binary world has developed in recent times. I think, on the whole, that while a considerable amount of time may be devoted to research, these days that time is often more peripheral to the research than actually doing it — writing grants, writing reports, advising and reviewing, supervising others — often we are more research as research facilitators than researchers. That there is not as much quality time for research may be indicated by the fact that three early career researchers have resigned from permanent posts in my Department in the last year or so, all citing not enough time for research.

Which leaves what can only be described as 'other things' — the committees, the emails, the online forms, the reports, the courses. In principle, of course, they may all be described as furthering teaching and research, but in practice they are the shadows of the real thing. What they do is fill the day (and, on many days, the evening as well).

Let's look at getting an hour's lecture out. When I started that was a case of preparing it (reading, thinking, writing notes), which could be a few hours and is probably much the same now. One would have given the students a handout at the beginning of term with some reading, and each lecture might have a handout with either complex figures or bullet points, typed and photocopied. Then one would write some outline and key points, draw some simple graphs, on overhead projector acetates. This may be buttressed by a few slides, usually prepared by the departmental or university photographic team. Then, off to lecture... and an hour later it was all over.

Now, the lecture needs a PowerPoint presentation (and that alone is a black hole for time spent looking for the perfect graphic and working out the best colour scheme), uploaded (at least) a day before the lecture, an abstract of the lecture uploaded to something, a reading list with the PDFs of the articles uploaded, possibly a recording uploaded beforehand these days, and if not, a recording done at the time, uploaded afterwards, answering emails from confused students ...and on it goes.

At the more masochistic end of academia, the lecture may be recorded and put online, and then an entirely separate hour devoted to discussing it (assuming the students have watched it), thus doubling the lecturers' time.

Where before one was an academic with a coloured pen set, now one is lecturer, graphics designer, film director, cameraman, TV presenter, IT expert, secretary, and occasional agony aunt. More significantly, the work for each lecture has probably quadrupled.

There is no doubt — at least I think there is no doubt — that the quality of teaching provided to students has increased. My poorly xeroxed black and white graphs do not really compete with fully referenced and slick PowerPoints and the opportunity to stop and start a recording as many times as you want. Universities are probably right to trumpet this change in what they no doubt call the learning experience, but they are wrong not to recognise the cost.

The cost is the time it takes out of the daily life of the academics. If teaching is supposed to take up about half our time, and the load has doubled or more, then that time has to come from somewhere — cricket time, research time, family time, all have to reduce commensurately. Academic life may be a game, but it is important to remember it is a zero-sum game — or at least should be.

Most businesses would probably go bankrupt if progress was measured in terms of producing the same product — a lecture — with massively more time and effort, but that is essentially what has happened in universities without anyone really noticing. Why? Because the costs were silently absorbed in academic staff time.

And this process applies not just to teaching, but to all the other activities we do. Grant applications — used to be, write a grant, show it to some knowledgeable colleagues, send it off and hope for the best. Now, at Cambridge at least, there are a series of internal deadlines and checks, so that a grant application may be processed and changed, possibly even rejected, many times before it even gets to a research council. A grant deadline in June may then have an internal deadline of March, stretching the process, and indeed the gap between internal and real deadline is likely to grow due to 'pressure of work' in the administration.

Kerchung, another addition in the cash till of time for the hard-working academic...

Postgraduate applications — once a rapid circulation of the papers, a few pithy comments, and then accept or reject. Now there are forms with endless criteria, bonus marks, and a space for comments on each justifying the points. Then an interview, involving at least two people, then meetings to agree rankings, then summaries of each case for higher entities...

Kerchung, another few (or many) hours gone...

Postdoctoral appointments would be a simple matter of an informal committee, a robust discussion of CVs, an interview and an offer and some apologetic letters to unsuccessful candidates. Now, it is HR directed, formal committees, the same questions to all, and complete adherence to a set of criteria that are likely to fade in the light of the real world of applicants, HR forms with scored and ranked candidates (carefully constructed to match the preferred outcome) and then, of course, the listing of all the reasons why the others were not appointed.

Kerchung, another few hours gone...

Examining — always a painful experience, for me at least, because one was aware of the serious responsibilities we were undertaking, but at least short and sharp. Increasingly, it is a continuous process of coursework assessment and feedback forms (please, not less than a page), and appeals.

Kerchung, another few hours gone...

Expenses — once a simple matter of a per diem, now we have to take a photograph of each receipt, upload it, enter the figures on spreadsheet and who knows what else.

Kerchung, another few hours gone...

Risk assessments, no I had better not go there.

Kerchung, another few days gone.

My point here is not the curmudgeonly one that this is managerialism gone mad, tempting as that is, but the practical outcomes of these changes for the people carrying them out. Simple tasks now just take longer and longer. Admittedly, there may have been a bit of slack in my cricket playing days, but there is none now, and each addition of tasks, each layer of process, each complex form adds minutes, hours and days to each bit of work. The effect of these is amplified by email, where (as discussed in a previous chapter) the ease of making requests can fill still further the day with amorphous blobs of activity.

These encrustations are not the core activities — the giving of a lecture, the writing of a paper, the selection of a candidate, the running of a lab or field project — but the peripheral and often surplus supports that have grown like barnacles around them.

Each may be beneficial and worthy — to students, to the auditing and accountability of the university, to compliance — but they come at a massive cost to the lumpen-academic. There are only so many hours in the day, and they were filled some time ago. Everything now either spills into the time we should be teaching or researching, or into our evenings and weekends.

And with each soulless, teaching-free, research-free hour that is added, three things happen. One is that the work of the average academic just grows and grows, invading terminally the life-work balance that is championed by all universities. Another is that morale slumps. A colleague of mine told me that he used an app to track exactly how he spent his time, but after a couple of months he abandoned it as it was too depressing. And the third is that people leave...

In her Admission Ceremony in 2022 the new Vice-Chancellor of Oxford, Irene Tracey, gave a very moving speech which included the following: 'we must find ways to shift the needle in your [academic staff] quality of life so that you can continue to deliver your best performance'.

A very promising signal, but it is not just a matter of shifting the needle to go faster or slower, but resetting it so that it measures what is important, not just in Oxford, but in Cambridge and all other universities. Too late for my cover drive, but very welcome.

9

INSTITUTIONS RUN ON THE MEMORIES OF PEOPLE

It is a truth universally acknowledged that memory declines with age. We all reach the age — if we're lucky — where recall becomes an increasingly hit and miss affair.

Names tend to go first — I'm down to half a dozen names of people I went to school with, and a few more I was an undergraduate with. Worse, of course, are the people I met yesterday, and can't quite put the name to the face. Worst is when I have to introduce them to someone else. No, on second thoughts, worst is introducing someone I have known for years, and the name just does not come.

Less significant, even amusing, is the loss of poetry. I was educated in a distant world where one was expected to learn screeds of poetry. I met an old school friend — one of the one's I remember — the other day, and he said that at around the age of 13 he had a bet with his teacher that he could learn the whole of — ah! forgotten the name of the poet, wait a minute...— Macaulay's 'Horatius' (thank you, Google). He lost with a mistake in the penultimate of seventy-odd stanzas. I was never in that league, but I could certainly do 'Once more unto the breach, dear friends, once more' from Shakespeare's *Henry V* with ease. What I have found, over the last decade, is that it has gradually gone away, line by line, from the bottom. I can still do as far as stiffening the sinews and summoning up the blood, but the rest is a blank. I suppose eventually it will just be 'once more'. That it is all there in Google rather than my head is something I am still pondering as a good thing or a bad thing.

But it is not just individuals who lose their memory. Institutions do as well. I suppose at 800 years and still aging, Cambridge might be forgiven for a bit of memory loss.

Indeed, some memory loss may be no bad thing, or there may be complete stasis and an inability to adapt to changing environments. As John Maynard Smith pointed out years ago, it might be thought that the perfect biological systems would eliminate mutation rates (a form of memory loss), but in practice they permit what might be considered the balance between stability and retaining the potential for change. I have a concern that, in Cambridge at least, that balance is threatened.

Institutional memory comes in many forms. The most stable, tablets of stone form, are the University Statutes, which used to appear in formidable dark blue volumes each year. These are effectively the constitution of the University, and can only be changed via the Privy Council — and no doubt the King is a bit busy with state affairs and his family at the moment to want too many such changes. The statutes are deliberately hard to change, to avoid whimsical shifts with each new wind of fashion. They are easily accessible online now, but they are seldom read by anyone. Their whiff of medievalism makes them seem remote from day-to-day life, rather than being the bedrock intended.

Below the Statutes are the Ordinances, and below these the Regulations, each a more malleable form of governance. In a way, the history of University governance is like a game of snakes and ladders, where activities occasionally become more important and climb the ladder from Regulation to Ordinance to Statute, but in these rapidly changing times it is more likely that they land on a snake and slither down in the other direction. Indeed, for practical purposes many higher order rules have been downgraded to a lower level, so that decisions that formally might have required approval from Regent House — the ultimate governance of the University — may now be approved by Council or some other body.

Whether this is the equivalent of the bonfire of EU regulations proposed by the Boris Johnson government, to be replaced by ministerial decrees, is for others to decide.

These are the formal institutional memory of the University, but they represent only a small fraction of what we might think of, in cognitive science terms, as the working memory. This is the product of two interrelated elements.

The first are the informal traditions that have evolved, the actual practices that are made up of the working rules and the moss of conventions that have grown over these — 'this is how it has always been done'.

The second is the actual memory and involvement of the people who carry out the institutional activities of the University in whom these conventions reside. It is the latter who have shaped, maintained and potentially lost the former.

The first, the informal traditions, are common to all institutions from the family to the nation state. We are largely unaware of these until we stay with another family or visit another country. The first Christmas with the in-laws is always an eye-opener. You open presents in your pyjamas? We are always dressed and drinking prosecco. You go to midnight mass? We are on the fourth bottle of prosecco. And so it goes.

Anyone trying to visit another country has to navigate the dilemmas of shake hands, one kiss, two kisses, three kisses, starting on the left, starting on the right, hugs, between men and women, between women, between men. And so it goes, usually even further.

The same is true for any university, and Oxbridge is particularly rich in such conventions, some bizarre and unfathomable. I once offered to shake hands with an elderly colleague, and he said, no, we had already met this term, so it was unnecessary. And don't even try and think about the hidden rules of a college. None of these are formally written down, and certainly not punishable in the breach beyond a raised eyebrow, but they are essential to the sense of shared knowledge, experience and intent. The customs of the tribe, as it were.

These do not just relate to social niceties, but how committees work and decisions are made. In my college all decisions are formal votes; on my former Faculty Board, I don't recall a single vote, and, in its high disciplinary diversity, it was accepted that larger entities would not outvote smaller ones.

In my former department, PhD applications were seen by all, but it was taken for granted that the supervisor would have a major if not the final say. Once merged with another department and new appointments were made, this practice was seen with horror, and potential supervisors were excluded from the process (in the surprising name of conflict of interest).

The clash of cultural traditions, old and new, was tectonic, but was not based on actual rules, but convention. I once challenged a Head of Department on the fact that a retiring colleague was involved in the selection of their successor, but when I took this to the central administration, I was told it was just a convention, and nothing could be done about its non-adherence.

However, these customs, norms, conventions are entirely dependent upon the informal institutional memory that resides in the individual academics, and it is not rocket science to work out that this is strongly correlated with length of service, and indeed educational experience. In my sub-discipline within a larger Department, now only two people have been in post longer than five years. And in the Department as a whole, only a small minority were undergraduates or graduates at Cambridge. Compare that with when I was an undergraduate, when all the lecturers and professors who taught me had been educated in some way or other, usually entirely, in Cambridge.

To return to the mutation rate model, the time I was a student was a situation of coelacanth proportions, with a virtually non-existent mutation rate. Change was glacial, because no one really knew of any alternatives, nor were particularly interested. Things just were. The broader and more diverse base now — not just educationally, but by gender and cultural background — is a much healthier situation. But there are always costs. Those costs are the loss of institutional memory. For a very successful university like Cambridge this is potentially a very great cost, because essentially, in terms of developing excellent students at all levels and being among the top-ranked research universities in the world, one must assume that the balance between change and stability embedded in the institutional memory was about right.

So what happens when institutional memory loss sets in? Does it matter? The memory is institutional knowledge, and with knowledge comes the power to do things, to do them efficiently, and indeed, the power to resist doing things as well. As fewer and fewer of the academic staff have the long-term knowledge, the wheel can be endlessly reinvented, often becoming more and more oval in the process.

Not knowing the unwritten customs of the tribe results in a loss of confidence, and an inability to challenge and shape and change the institution from below, and to resist change from above. Fear of not knowing the unwritten customs must at least be partly responsible for the reluctance of academics to engage with governance. Cambridge prides itself on being a bottom-up university, but with each year this becomes less and less true as the memories are lost at the bottom, and confidence is replaced by the oft-heard 'am I allowed?'.

There is another risk as well. If people do not know the unwritten rules, there is an irresistible temptation to write them down. These do not have the power of the statutes, ordinances and regulations, but websites are now replete with guidelines, best practice, steps to follow, boxes to check. The sources and authorities of these are usually invisible, but they trump the unwritten customs for being written down. And, of course, they come from above, not from below, and if academic tenure is short, administrative tenure is likely to be shorter still, and institutional memory shallow. So, what better than to get the memory off the shelf from somewhere else.

Cultures — and Cambridge and Oxford are ancient cultures — die when they lose their memory, just as they die if they do not adapt and change. The balance of change and stability in the evolution of an institution, just as in organisms, can be fragile, and I think that fragility is all too real at the moment. Institutions are made of memories, work through their memories, and their memories reside in people.

Widely shared institutional memory must be the basis for a genuine bottom-up university.

10

BOOK, BENCH, BUSY, BUSH AND BRAIN THE DIVERSE SPECIES OF ACADEMIA

Most of my Ivory Flats commentaries are written in the cosy environment of Cambridge, but this one has been brewing in the deserts of northern Kenya, where I have been for a while doing fieldwork. It is an excessively hot environment, with temperatures often reaching 40 degrees, but it is also dry. The people of Turkana — indeed of the whole of the Horn of Africa — have been suffering for a drought for nearly three years, and the costs are high. Water is limited, food in short supply, and grazing for animals virtually non-existent. This is always a hard land, but it seems desperately so now. We have been working here for fifteen years, and so seeing the stress to our many friends is heartbreaking.

Doing fieldwork in Africa turns one's mind to diversity, for it is all around one here — the diversity of cultures and languages, the diversity of the plants and animals, indeed, even human genomic diversity which is greater than that across the whole of Eurasia.

And of course, diversity is a word we hear more and more frequently. One would have to have been living in complete isolation not to be aware that diversity is a big issue in UK universities at the moment, and it is a rare soul who has not taken a course on equality and diversity, probably several times. There is no doubt that the focus on cultural and socio-economic diversity is a huge priority, and has done much to widen the student and staff profile of universities, to their benefit.

But diversity comes in many dimensions, and I have been thinking about the other ways in which universities are diverse, and musing on whether there are some endangered species out there.

Oxford, Cambridge and Durham are unusual, if not unique, in having colleges as one of their forms of diversity, but although I shall probably get run out of my college for saying so, they are not as different one from another as they like to think. I can navigate the mysteries of SCRs and Directors of Studies meetings (and dinners) with ease. Certainly, from a distance they are peas in a pod. No, the real university diversity is by discipline and department. Drop a linguist in the biochemistry department and they will be completely lost, and vice versa, of course.

This is not just a matter of knowing which reagents or phonemes do what, nor of being distant disciplines, but the culture of place. Excavate into any merged department or Faculty — no matter how long ago — and the old fissures are easy enough to see. My own Faculty had three Departments that were shot-gunned together against our wishes (so much for a bottom-up university) in 2010, but the boundaries remained as visible as ever — indeed, the marriage was dissolved within a few years, perhaps annulled, as there was never the remotest chance of consummation except in the fantasies of the 'senior management' who pushed it through.

Disciplines are, of course, divided by subject matter and knowledge, united by shared ideas and histories. The eyes that glaze on a topic that goes beyond one's comfort zone are a well-known phenomenon around any university. 'How interesting!', one says as the mathematician raptures about a torus, or the sociologist about Durkheim. There are, though, deeper divisions, that relate not to what we do, but how we do it.

It might seem that the way to explore this form of diversity is to start listing disciplines and all their idiosyncrasies, possibly even alphabetically, and we can link them easily to the world of cinema and television to know all there is to know — Anglo-Saxon (just watch the *Last Kingdom*), Archaeology (*Indiana Jones and the Raiders of the Lost Ark*), Astronomy (*Star Wars*), ... Zoology (David Attenborough, of course). Alternatively, one can go down the well-trodden path of humanities, social sciences and natural sciences, and rehearse C.P. Snow's *Two* (now three) *Cultures*. Cornford's *Microcosmographia* introduced five species of politically-minded academics — Conservative Liberals, Liberal Conservatives, Non-Placets (the most conservative who vote against everything on principle!), Adullamites (another class of anti-reformers), and Angry Young Men.

However, I have a different classification in mind. Giving in to the overwhelming temptation to alliterate, there are probably five basic academic species or cultures — *Book*, *Brain*, *Bench*, *Busy* and *Bush*. These meander across disciplines and sadly fail to recognise the importance of universities' silos of Schools, Faculties and Departments; you will find Bushes in departments ranging from Classics to Chemistry, and Brains in Maths and Philosophy.

But these academic species offer better insights into what people actually do, what motivates them to get up in the morning, or to inspire others — and how the managerial drive for uniformity fails to embrace this form of diversity.

The *Books* are the dwellers in libraries and archives, detectives or lovers of the written word. They may be found tracking down the lost accounts of some Suffolk sheep-shearer from the fourteenth century, enjoying a glass of Pinot Grigio after a day delving into a Venetian love letter, semi-interred in a library basement, or more likely these days, wading through piles of PDFs. Knowledge and advances in knowledge come from finding sources, reading, sifting primary and secondary sources, and unravelling the palimpsests of previous research.

The *Benches* are the laboratory dwellers, troglodytic characters surrounded by machines and pipettes, or sitting on a mountain observatory staring at a remote star, or chasing protons in Switzerland, or more likely these days, in front of a computer screen like the rest of us.

The *Busys* are the real-worlders of academia, the lawyers, economists, engineers, regulars on the London trains, popping in and out of Westminster, Whitehall, British Gas or the law courts. They exude an air of impatience with the demands of their university life, rushing out from the pillars of the business school or the modernism of the Law Faculty to change our mortgage rates or explain the world on the *Today Programme*.

The *Bushes* are the people who are never in Cambridge, or at least say they're not. 'Sorry, can't make the meeting, I'm in the field.' At their worst they wear their dirty field boots in seminars to remind you how tough they are, just back from the wilds. The wilds, of course, could be the Cambridge Fens as easily as Antarctica. Bushes come in an amazing variety of forms, from those who are getting ill in the Amazon to those who are wandering the streets of Newcastle with a clipboard. They know there are important new things to find 'out there', but often, it has to be said, the means — getting away — is as important as the ends.

And the *Brains* are the thinkers, working it all out from first principles, whether in the moral maze or the multiverse. Seldom seen, seldom understood.

There is clearly overlap — an English professor wandering lonely as a cloud around the Lake District pondering Wordsworth might count as a member of the Bushes, while an archivist delicately separating leaves of an ancient manuscript would probably qualify for Bench status. Even the most weather-beaten of the Bushes must occasionally have to venture bravely into a library, and are often only too glad to go on television just like a Busy. Benches must venture out to collect samples if they can't get a Bush to do it for them. Sometimes a Brain alone is not sufficient. Some are natural hybrids — medics are probably both Benches and Busys. The Busys do it all anyway.

And each is viewed by the others through a warped and stereotypical lens, a classic case of in-group/out-group rivalry. To the Benches, the Books are self-indulgently spending their time reading, and anyone can do that, can't they? To the Books, the Benches are boring night owls, myopically staring down microscopes or mixing noxious chemicals that are going to destroy the planet. The Busys roll their eyes at the irrelevance of Thomas Aquinas today, and wish the Bushes would dress more smartly. As at least a part-time Bush myself, I work in a scorpion-infested desert in high temperatures and sleep in a tent, but am inevitably met on my return — especially in the winter — with sarcastic comments about being on holiday again ('alright for some, I have six lectures and ten committees today').

There is also a hierarchy to these groups, and each knows well the pecking order. Unsurprisingly, of course, it is different for all. Benches are proud of their rigour, objectivity and machines that go ping, as well as their self-identified relevance to the problems of the real world. The Books are intellectuals, and so look down on all the rest as essentially technicians. The Bushes are the hard men and women of the real world, risking life and limb in search of new discoveries of beetles, earthquakes, kinship systems and fossil fragments, and tend to view the rest of academia as sheltered milksops. The Busys are naturally too busy to notice there are others. The Brains live above it all.

The point about this idiosyncratic way of looking at academic diversity is that it reflects how people spend their daily lives, schedule their months and years, prioritise their time, identify their goals, find satisfaction, and see themselves in the University Universe. And each of these is very different, requiring different schedules, different support, different resources, but similar respect.

Real people do not have goals, missions, deliverables in a vague bullet-pointed list that they look at respectfully each morning, but a love of their particular way of finding things out and doing the things involved in that search — in a way, their craft.

For research and teaching there is an inevitable knot that ties the means and the ends. I might have a deep interest in those fourteenth-century sheep-shearers, but no inclination to work in an archive for hours and hours. Others might love the excitement of finding a fossil, but are terrified of scorpions. That entanglement between what we do and how we do it is at the core of being an academic. And it can be lost too — the fieldwork becomes too hard with age or family or both, the bench becomes monotonous or automated. That loss is probably the first step on the road to becoming a university manager.

And mentioning university managers, as was inevitable in Ivory Flats, leads us back to diversity. Centralisation has demanded uniformity of treatment and process — no doubt a noble goal, but one rich with hidden dangers. Looked at from the centre, it must seem that the most common and so typical academic is either a Book or a Bench — sitting in a library or a laboratory. And it is a short step from there to the expectation that the same needs and demands can be applied across the species diversity. For the Benches comes the expectations that they must bring in lots of money to pay for research assistants, and from the Books that they will be dutifully working in Cambridge and not straying too far, not requiring much money, and so propping up the institution. The model (and desired) academic becomes a locally-dwelling cash machine.

But this one size does not fit all. Some people need to be away a lot (Bushes), some people simply don't need money but time (Brains), some people publish big impenetrable tomes (Books), others myriads of citable journal papers (Benches); some people go on television (Busys), others will wait years to divulge their views (Brains).

The Books and the Benches can no doubt produce elegant and beautiful accounts all following the preferred provider routes with ease; others, such as us Bushes in Turkana, have scraps of paper covering the purchase of a goat (alive, so capital cost, but eaten, so rapidly depreciated and literally a consumable, please resubmit). Risk assessments are trivial for a saunter to Dublin for a conference, slightly more daunting for a trip to Iran.

And I am sure, in the minds of the stressed people who have to process the torn receipts and work out which snakes are really dangerous, the outliers of the system just appear to be difficult and not very cost-effective. So much easier to have a world of Benches and Books. Even the Busys are a bit of a risk as they may say something controversial, and the Brains don't earn any money! And so the impediments to being different grow everywhere.

Diversity has become a word with an ironically narrow meaning, but we should not forget that at the core of what we do as academics there is also a dimension of diversity that is central to our being. *How* we do things is as essential as what we do, and so achieve both our own individual goals and ultimately those of the university as well.

It is probably the case that all institutions from the family to the state must grapple with the balance between uniformity and diversity, and the outcome will vary, and it is equally true that the greater the centralisation of an institution, the greater the pendulum will swing towards uniformity, as it does now.

Diversity of academic style also challenges the tree-like organograms that are there to simplify the life of the central administration. It would be so much easier if all the Bushes were in the biological sciences, all the Brains in maths, all the Busys in the Business School, and all the Books in the humanities. But it doesn't work that way, meaning that each branch of the university's tree must be able to support and cater for each species, something that can be an administrative stretch.

As I see it, a centralising monoculture is pushing out the delightful local ecosystems in which the multiple weird and wonderful species of academic thrive. They do not need just the basic nutrients of research and teaching, but support for how they do things as well, nurturing the means as well as the ends. It is the different habitats and niches of academia, our varied ways of life, that make our working lives pleasurable and successful.

Now, back to check for scorpions.

11

FEARFUL ASYMMETRY: THE END OF THE PEER SHOW

If there is evidence that parts of the English language were explicitly designed by a xenophobic committee to confuse foreigners, it is the word 'peer'. Only a cunning and possibly diabolic mind could use the same word to mean 'equals' and that most superior of groups, the aristocracy. If you add the homophone 'pier' to the list, exasperation is complete. 'The peer is drinking with his peer on the pier.'

However, foreigners, despite Brexit, need despair no longer, as the word is rapidly losing its dual meaning, and the usage that implies nothing but a hierarchical relationship is now dominant. Notions of equality in the word are rapidly slipping into what lexicographers call archaic.

Universities have always prided themselves on an ethos of equality. College Fellows at Oxford and Cambridge are perhaps the epitome of this — a Fellow is a Fellow, regardless of whether they have been there since the Oxford and Cambridge Act of 1926, or just arrived from Ulan Bator. Even Heads of Oxbridge colleges are in deep trouble if they make the mistake of taking titles like Master, President, Principal too literally. Across universities as a whole, equality is largely taken for granted. A senior lecturer (as was) has no authority over a lecturer, and the title Professor bestows no rights to tell anyone else what to do, tempting as it sometimes is.

Authority lies in specific and usually temporary appointments — Head of Department, Pro-Vice-Chancellor, and so on, but even these titles give only limited authority and should — in principle — be constrained by being effectively chairs of boards and councils, rather than chief executives. If there was ever a peer show, it was universities.

No doubt any student reading this might be shouting out, but what about us? Not exactly peers. True, but even then, the relationship between lecturers and professors and students is fluid, with little direct authority beyond the examination process and more extreme situations where disciplinary actions have to be invoked. Fortunately, these last are very rare, and for the most part in my experience, relationships between teacher and student are relatively relaxed. I still balk a bit whenever a first year student whom I have never met comes up to me and says 'Hi, Rob', but the routes out of this situation are so prone to pomposity that I generally grin and bear it.

The most explicit context for the meeting of equals is the peer review system. This is such a jewel in the crown of academic life that even journalists will now state whether an article has been peer-reviewed, meaning received the certificate of quality, even truth, by its peers. The peer review system — where grant applications and journal papers are scrutinised by one's equals, is a wonderful meeting of minds, where applicant or author can fruitfully exchange ideas and discuss constructive criticism with expert and open-minded colleagues in one's own field. These interactions are usually a joy and pleasure, untainted by inequality or competitiveness.

I can hear hollow laughs from any author of a journal paper reading that last paragraph. One only has to do an internet search, especially on Twitter, for 'Reviewer 2' to have some idea of the depth of feeling of stress, anxiety and frustration that is caused by the so-called peer review system.

I have seen the shock and loss of confidence in young researchers getting their first bad review, and I am not sure it isn't even worse that aged academics like myself have become so inured to these often caustic comments that we just shrug our shoulders and move on.

In both cases it is a loss of the dream that publishing your research is supposed to be.

It is easy enough to find both highly scientific and very amusing critiques of the unfairness and inadequacy of the peer review system, but there is a deeper structural issue that is often neglected. 'Peer review' is supposed to use the word peer in its 'equals' meaning. Unfortunately, it has morphed into its more lordly one.

The author is like a feudal peasant in supplication to the courtiers (reviewers) and editors (kings and queens), desperately hoping for a favourable glance, and worrying about a sudden execution looming (rejection). It is a rare reviewer who seriously sees themselves on the same level as the author or grant applicant. They are more than happy to be judge, jury and executioner, and like all good axemen (I think they were all men in those days) they are hooded to avoid recognition.

Given that many of the reviewers will also (hopefully) submit papers themselves, and moan about the system as well, how do we account for these Jekyll and Hyde personae? It may simply be one of the outlets for the overworked and stressed academic who is yet again being diverted from what they want to do, but they have chosen the wrong person to take their frustration out on. I am sure it is sometimes jealousy and competitiveness, and in young reviewers an overdose of youthful criticality. In older ones, conservative grumpiness. However, I think there is more to it than just these irritants.

It is perhaps a bit of a stretch, but I am reminded of aspects of the famous Stanford experiment. In this extremely unethical experiment, volunteers were randomly assigned as guards or prisoners in a role-playing situation. Over a period of less than a week the guards became increasingly authoritarian and abusive, and the prisoners more anxious and rebellious. Zimbardo's aim was to show how people conformed to the roles they were assigned, and where these involved authority, how inhibitions were shed. Exactly the same people, in different circumstances, would behave entirely differently.

Fortunately, Reviewer 2 does not imprison authors, but the principle is the same — a position of anonymous or protected authority does not seem to inspire the sympathy, support and empathy that should characterise a proper peer-peer system.

Of course, the peer review system is much older than the problems with Reviewer 2 and the general disillusion with the system. What has changed? There are many factors. For once, I can't think of a way of blaming email, but the growth of anonymity in the world of social media that has led to high levels of abuse may have had a broader infectious effect. The increased competitiveness of the academic world and the pressure to publish must be a large part of the problem, and the gatekeepers have become more defensive in response.

However, I think there are two changes in university life that have played an even larger role. The first is the sheer size of academia. In 2012 there were more than 100,000 doctoral students in the UK[1]; in 1975–6 4,815 people graduated with PhDs in the UK[2]. This demographic expansion has many plus sides, especially relating to equality of opportunity, but it also means that there is far less of a sense of community. That smaller, closed community might not have been an entirely good thing — 'I know Jones is a jolly good chap, so I'm sure the paper is worth publishing' — but it also meant that unnecessary vindictiveness was harder to hide. In the vast, international academic world today, that is no longer true, and we know that empathy and sympathy decline with social distance.

The other is the growing sense of impotence that university lecturers and professors now have. With less and less autonomy, freedom of action, control over their lives, being Reviewer 2 is one of the few outlets left to achieve a sense of control and authority.

I have grown depressed by the demise of a system that was designed to bring quality through equality. I have cowered too long under the whip of Reviewers 1, 2 and 3 (up to 9 in the case of one paper). We have all, I am sure, expressed the commonest of academic lies —no, not 'I haven't quite finished reading your essay, I'll get it back to you later today' — but 'Dear Editor, I would like to thank you and the anonymous reviewers for your helpful and constructive comments on my paper'.

This year, I finally turned and withdrew a paper that was accepted subject to revision, saying that I felt the gap between myself and the reviewers was too great to bridge. I should have done it years ago.

Moaning about the peer review is now standard fodder, but I think what is neglected is that it is not the source of the problem, but actually just one symptom of a deeper loss of a peer-based system.

The title professor may bestow no authority, and so be entirely consistent with the peer-based organisation of the traditional university, but many new titles are emerging with a much more ominous ring. Cambridge is now replete with Directors of this, that and the other, and presumably their job is to direct rather than to profess. Occasionally one sees vice-chancellors referred to as CEOs, and I am sure there are Chief Operating Officers lurking in some universities now. Cambridge used to have collaborative sounding titles like Registrar, Treasurer, Academic

Secretary, all very senior people, but these are gradually being replaced. I know of at least one Cambridge college that changed their Senior Tutor for a Director of Education. Organograms are the visual representation of hierarchy — the 'Director' is always at the top of the page.

There is no reason why these titles should be more than just an updating of old-fashioned terms to something more modern and dynamic, but they have, to my mind, a whiff of authoritarianism about them, and many are imports from the world of business, where peer-based egalitarianism is not notable. Less peers, and more 'the Peer'.

This does not seem to me to be a path towards academic utopia. Give people a sense — or title — of authority and not surprisingly the temptation to use it will be overwhelming, and even more so if their aims are at risk of being frustrated by those who think that although there is an inevitable cost in a more democratic process — yes, I'm thinking of those endless committee meetings — it is a cost worth paying to ensure that we remain institutions based on peers rather than a self-appointed peerage.

We see this shift all too clearly in the world around us, so while it is not surprising that universities are succumbing to the same trends, a little bit of civic resistance is no bad thing.

Peer to peer relationships are central to university life, whether it is at arm's length through the grant and journal reviewing process, or more directly in the relationship between academics and the administration. They are, though, being eroded. Any peer-based system demands a symmetry between participants, something absent in the directives from senior management teams to even the most senior of professors.

I am reminded of Richard Dawkins and John Krebs's 'life-dinner principle'[3], one of my favourite evolutionary models. Why does the rabbit run faster than the fox? Because the rabbit is running for its life, the fox only for its dinner. This asymmetry powers their co-evolutionary trajectories. For Reviewer 2, it is just dinner; for the early career researcher submitting their first paper, it is life. For the administrator sending down another task for the academics to do it is one more decision taken; for the academic it is an eternity of extra work and constraint.

'Restore symmetry' might be a suitably intellectual slogan for the revolution, otherwise it really will be the end of the peer show.

12

THE GREAT UNIVERSITY SUBSIDY SCANDAL

Being a *Guardian* reader, I don't know if the *Telegraph* still gets letters from 'Disgusted of Tunbridge Wells', but if they did, I might write one myself.

> Dear Sir,
>
> I am appalled to discover that universities, well known as the home of the work-shy, as well as students, are luxuriating in endless rounds of subsidises, while we hard-working pensioners struggle to find the money for the second G & T.
>
> Yours truly,
>
> DoTW

Horror of horrors — creeping socialism, pampered academics, and so on and so forth. But of course, universities are subsidised in the sense that they receive financial support from the government, as of course they should. Yet, there is indeed an unknown form of subsidy in the system — the extent to which universities are subsidised by their own academic staff. This is the great university subsidy scandal that I have in mind.

Let me count the ways. I can start with something relatively small and trivial — mobile phones. It is my understanding (alright, suspicion) that in any university administration there are quite a number of university mobile phones, phones paid for by the University to be used for official business. I am sure that these are completely necessary as so much work must, these days, be carried out by mobile, not to mention monitoring emails and finding information.

But I have yet to come across an academic who has a University phone. Perhaps, this is because they don't do any university business? Of course they do, but there is what should probably be called unconscious bias involved in this. We talk to colleagues (all over the world) about research, about collaborations, about teaching and ideas, about students. We double-factor identify ourselves using our personal phones when logging in to University admin websites to write student reports, etc. Actually we double-factor identify ourselves endlessly.

But somehow, despite the fact that the university is, as they say, a place of education and research, this does not really count as 'university business'. Presumably this is a vestige of the idea that, at heart, we do this stuff (research and teaching) because we enjoy it, and so should be quite happy to pay for the privilege. Subsidy one.

Keeping in the digital world, let's move on to WFH — working from home. In this case academics have been world pioneers, having worked from home long before it became fashionable. There are many reasons for that, from those who want to get some work done to those who do not. Many has been the departmental secretary who has had to tell some long-suffering student that they haven't seen Dr Bloggs for weeks. But now WFH is an acceptable mode of operation for most staff.

There is clearly the expectation that digital contact is

maintained, and equally, that the resources to work efficiently are at home. This means good quality internet and Wi-Fi access, camera, microphone, etc., and this comes at a cost. My wife is also an academic, and although we have never calculated it, my guess is that most of our internet usage is related to work (how sad!). But we can add this to the list. Indeed, I seem to remember getting advice about the types of desks, chairs and screens I needed to work safely at home (danger money?), but no mention that the university might pay for them. Subsidy two.

These are what might be considered hidden subsidies, as there is no observable cash involved. However, there are some where real hard dosh is spent. Except for those of us who are not, we are a sociable bunch on the whole, and food and drink are the lubricants of ideas, of writing papers, of discussing the wonders or horrors of the last seminar, and bringing students and academics together as part of the process of both being inclusive and encouraging young people.

After a seminar, visiting speakers are taken to pubs and dinners. In any other profession these would be business expenses, but in universities, while it is possible to claim for the speaker (who, in my experience, often finds the hassle of reclaiming expenses too great!), the others dutifully throw their debit cards into the hat, and often the more senior people pay for any students there.

External examiners, who are paid a pittance for two or three days' work and travel, are usually pleased to anoint with alcohol the heads of the happy student after the viva (while the supervisor may have bought a bottle of brandy for the less happy ones).

We travel to conferences (almost certainly at some cost to ourselves even if there are some funds available) and there is no doubt that the lunches and dinners (breakfasts as well if you are in the USA) are places where serious work gets done. I exaggerate, of course, because this is not universal, and vice-chancellors scraping a living, do get an entertainment allowance.

I should perhaps declare a conflict of interest here, as

Oxbridge colleges do subsidise some of these activities, perhaps wisely recognising their importance, but this is a luxury only possible outside formal university structures. Anyway, subsidy three.

Larger if less permanent subsidies occur for those who do fieldwork. Getting an institutional credit card is generally harder than the UK getting a vote in the Eurovision song contest, so most expenditure is racked up on personal accounts, and then reimbursed. This can soon mount up to thousands of pounds, something that few can afford, and reimbursement can take months. Imagine a lab director paying for all their reagents on their credit cards, and waiting to be paid back — that is the lot of the fieldworker. Subsidy four.

Then there are the subsidies at either end of the academic career. At the starting end, more and more of the small class teaching (seminars, tutorials, supervisions) are done by PhD students, not the best remunerated groups, or by those who have recently finished doctorates and are on the hunt for their first step on the academic ladder.

These are all either actual or virtual zero-hour contracts, which in effect means that the poorest of our community are subsidising the university. This is partly the fact that the pay is for the contact hours only, not including the time it takes to prepare and assess work (always more from those starting), and partly as there are none of the additional costs an employer would pay to a real employee — sickness benefit, parental leave, holiday pay, national insurance.

At the other end of the scale, I am sure I am not alone in having retired and then asked to come back and lecture, mark exams, etc. While this is not the same level of exploitation as for the early career researchers, it does testify to the fact that the university academic body is understaffed, and so yet another way in which the silent subsidies operate. Subsidy five.

And now we come to the one that puts all the others into

the shade — the number of hours necessary for an academic to do their work. I have despaired about this before, but largely in terms of stress, morale and the work-life balance, but there are also financial elements to consider. While it is true — as far as I know — that contracts for academics do not specify the number of hours ('just get the work done, there's a good chap'), there are realistic expectations.

Working weeks vary across Europe, from 32.2 in the Netherlands to 40 in Greece, and across sectors, with agriculture, forestry and fishing industries topping the list at 41.8 hours[1]. Lawyers, bankers and junior doctors are likely to push these numbers up, although some — but not junior doctors — are well remunerated for it.

Full-time contracts for non-academic staff are usually around 36 hours per week. But most academics work far more hours than this — evenings and weekends are seldom work-free, and I suspect that many if not most do not take their full holiday entitlement. While people might say, they are choosing to work because they find Sanskrit inscriptions or coding in Python so fascinating, that is irrelevant, as research is a core part of the job... a bit like saying that accountants aren't really working because they like spreadsheets.

The outcome is that universities are getting far more for their buck than they deserve. Essentially, universities are receiving a Rolls Royce service for the price of a second-hand Ford Mondeo. So let us play some fantasy models. Let us say that between the extra hours over 36 a week (15 perhaps, far less than the not unreasonable 100 hours a week of Mary Beard) and a week's holiday not taken, academics are doing about 40% more work than they are being paid for. Take into account that salaries are some 20% down in real terms compared to 2008, then universities are getting about 50% of their academic labour for free.

What ruthless business wouldn't dream for this level subsidy — it makes Amazon look like model employers. Alright, that exercise hardly makes it as even a back of the envelope calculation, but at half that level it does amount to a whopping subsidy. Subsidy number six.

To be fair, responsibility for much of this does not lie with 'The University', for it (generically) is constrained in many ways by levels of government funding and rules governing fees, but at the sharp end it feels the same. In small and large ways, the academic staff on whom all universities depend for their core activities of teaching and research are subsidising their institutions very substantially, mostly invisibly and largely unrecognised.

As an evolutionary biologist, I spend much of my time trying to estimate the costs of adaptations — a large brain brings many benefits, but the costs in terms of energy, metabolism, and parental care are enormous. Flight is wonderful, but the costs come in terms of brittle bones to reduce weight. Searching for hidden costs is second nature.

Much of the progress and many of the changes in universities in the last decade have been borne by the hidden costs for the academic staff. Many are intangible and relate to job satisfaction and morale, but these are real economic ones that affect not just the individuals currently in employment (and on strike), but also the ability of universities to recruit. Quiet resignations, real resignations and non-applications are on the rise.

Universities are not the ultimate driver of this situation, and they themselves are victims of a prolonged period of government cuts, and so they end up trapped between a rock and a soft place (academic staff). However, the loss of a shared experience between management and the academic staff has meant that what should be seen as a common problem is easily escalated into 'them' and 'us'.

If 'Disgusted of Tunbridge Wells' has read this far, they would probably be happily saying that this shows academics simply aren't the clever clogs they think they are. Perhaps they are right.

13

ARE YOU SURE THAT BOAT IS SAFE, MR DARWIN?

A favourite academic quotation of mine is that 'knowledge is bought with assumptions'. Very true, but it is also bought with effort, and sometimes that effort involves risks. Reading the memoirs of early scientific travellers — Wallace, Humboldt, Shackleton — is enough to make most of us check the house for mosquitoes or turn up the central heating. Herbert, the brother of Alfred Wallace, co-founder with Charles Darwin of the theory of evolution, died of yellow fever after travelling with Wallace in the Amazon[1], and reading the records of the explorers looking for the source of the Nile is a nervous person's nightmare, as they are constantly suffering fevers, or attacked by animals or people. We tend to think of Darwin as an old man with a long white beard, wrapped up warm in his house in Kent, but as Janet Browne says in her wonderful biography[2], as a young man he loved the outdoor life and the adventures of riding, hunting, exploring. The voyage of the *Beagle* was for Darwin, and all his comrades, an extraordinarily exciting and risky venture. It is probably fair to say that many people, usually young, seek out risks.

Seeking risks, or being prepared to take extraordinary risks for the sake of new knowledge, is increasingly at odds with modern institutional attitudes. Part of that is driven by a natural concern for the well-being of people in their care, partly by the normalisation of the relatively low level of risk in British society today. (All risks are relative to some sort of baseline. If you live constantly in an environment of a very pleasant 22C, then a drop of 10 degrees is a major risk to one's well-being; if you live in a war zone then that would not even register.) And part of it comes from the strong instinct for institutions to protect their reputation (and reduce their, or the insurance company's, own risks, usually financial).

Risk avoidance is certainly a good thing (ask any parent), but sometimes risks are not just faced and tolerated, sometimes they are embraced and welcomed. One of the early pioneers of psychology, Henry Head, had the radial and external cutaneous nerves in his arm severed, so that he and his colleague W.H.R. Rivers could investigate nerve recovery[3] (I will not mention their other experiments as they will have male readers anxiously crossing their legs). The great biologist J.B.S. Haldane spent some of the First World War standing behind walls while his father blew them up, testing the efficacy — or not — of the protection they gave. Risk-averse and risk-prone behaviours are both natural human behaviours. Time, places, contexts, personality, social norms, economics will shape and favour each, but they probably cannot happily coexist.

The clash of perspectives is unavoidable, and unresolvable. For the most part the two do not meet, but through a strange compression of time two periods separated by nearly two hundred years came together and a 22-year-old Charles Darwin was interviewed about his risk assessment form and proposal before going on HMS *Beagle*. A record of it has slipped through a wormhole for us to witness...

CD = Charles Darwin
Int = Interviewer

Int: Ah, come in, sit down... Charles is it, or do you prefer Charlie?
CD: Charles, please.
Int: Thank you for coming to meet us. We called you in as we have been reading your very interesting — indeed challenging — proposal, and especially the risk assessment that goes with it. We do have a few questions.
CD: Of course.
Int: Now, if we understand this correctly, you propose to go round the world and carry out researches into natural history. You'll be working for a Captain Fitzroy.
CD: Yes, that's right.
Int: How did you come to get this position? Was it advertised?
CD: Er, no, Professor Henslow suggested to Captain Fitzroy that I would be a good person, being a naturalist and a gentleman.
Int: I see... So there was no advertisement, no interviews, no other candidates... a bit old-fashioned, don't you think? A problem for Human Resources, I suppose. Let's get started.

Now, we take mental health very seriously, and our first task is to make sure that this is not a trip that will endanger your mental health. We understand this is the second voyage of HMS *Beagle*. Does that provide us with the assurance we need that mental health will not be an issue?
CD: Er, I believe the captain, Pringle Stokes, committed suicide during the first voyage.
Int: Not a very good start, Charlie, is it? We had better put that down as a 'No'. Now, let's move on to transport and accommodation. We understand the 'project vehicle' is HMS *Beagle*, a Cherokee-class brig — an unfortunate name in this day and age. How many people will be on it?
CD: Sixty-five sailors and ten supernumeraries like myself.

Int: I see. ...And how many rooms?
CD: Well. There's a cabin I will share with Captain Fitzroy, the other officers share, and most of the rest are in a single room, I think.
Int: I believe the boat is only 27 metres long. That's a lot of people in such a small space. Not very hygienic.
CD: Ship.
Int: Ship?
CD: It's a ship, not a boat.
Int: Boats, ships... For the purposes of risk assessments all water-borne craft are considered to be boats. We have to keep it simple for the database. Now, we understand that boat journeys can be quite rough. Do you have any relevant experience of sailing?
CD: No.
Int: I think, then, that you should probably take a course before travelling. I do hope you don't get sea-sick...[4]
You have left blank anything about other modes of transport. We assume you will travel on land, so we need more details here — owners' names, vehicle details.
CD: I think they'll be mules, horses, perhaps donkeys. I don't know their names, I'm afraid.
Int: Very well. Please supply these as soon as you have them.
Let's turn to your study area. From your previous answers, I'll take it as read that you do not have any relevant field experience, but you have listed the study area as Cape Verde Islands, Bahia, Rio de Janeiro and surrounding areas, Montevideo and surrounding area, the Falkland Islands, Tierra del Fuego, large parts of Chile and Peru, the Galapagos Islands — never heard of them — New Zealand, bits of Australia (undefined), and Cape Town in South Africa. This seems to be very ambitious for someone so inexperienced. I'm afraid we will need detailed plans and maps for all these areas.
CD: But they're unexplored by scientists — that's why we're going there.

Int: I understand that, but that makes it all very high risk, and generally we prefer early career researchers to work in areas for which we already have substantial knowledge. What exactly do you plan to do — 'naturalising' and 'geologising' were not very helpful responses.
CD: I'm going to look at all the geology, sort of see whether the land has risen and fallen, or the sea. I'm going to study volcanoes, and do the stratigraphy of all the places we visit. As Captain Fitzroy will be doing depth surveys for the Admiralty, I shall sample the animals in the sea as we travel. On land I want to go and look for fossils, as well as collect samples of plants and animals for me to study later. All that diversity will be useful in some way. I'm not certain what to do in the Galapagos Islands, but I'm sure something will come to me.
Int: So, geology, marine biology, palaeontology and zoology. A bit broad, don't you think? A bit ambitious. We need more details about methods and so on, so that we can assess any health and safety concerns we might have. What happens, for example, if while you're looking for animals you get bitten by some poisonous bug, and get Chagas disease for example?[5]
CD: I don't know.
Int: And other dangers — suppose a volcano erupts — do you have an exit strategy?
CD: I'm sure that won't happen.[6]
Int: And aren't there earthquakes where there are volcanoes?
CD: Sometimes, but it's rare.[7]
Int: Now, let's turn to accommodation on land. You don't seem to have provided, as required by the forms, the lists, addresses and plans of all accommodation during the project, remembering that AirBnB is strongly discouraged.
CD: Well, I don't really know where I'll be staying, and for how long. It all depends on what we find, what Captain Fitzroy wants to do, what is happening in the area.
Int: I think, Charlie, that you'll find a Gantt chart helpful for

you to plan your time more effectively, and will allow you to fill in all the contact details and locations that we will need. Now, we need to get you to set check-in times. You'll have to check in with designated personnel at fixed points, so that we know you're safe.
CD: That'll be very difficult — sort of depends on how the wind blows. Whenever I can, I'll send letters with passing boats returning to England, or leave them with people in the towns we visit, and someone will pick them up and pass them on, I'm sure.
Int: That really does look very haphazard and unreliable.
I see you have put 'may be expected to take part in military operations' in response to questions about special hazards.
CD: Yes, South America is a pretty volatile area, I understand, but I'm sure it will be exciting to walk with Pistols & Cutlass through the streets of a Town.[8]
Int: Hmm, not sure that is quite the answer we were looking for. Well, I'm afraid we have run out of time. We would have liked to talk more, especially about research permits, local collaboration, and this strange matter of someone called Jeremy Button, but I don't think that is likely to change our views. Ultimately, of course, it's up to the University's insurers.
By the way, we consider 'about five years' to really be too long and too vague for your answer to 'duration of the project'. We'll provide you with feedback so that you can revise your forms.
CD: How long will that take? The tide is turning, the ship — er, boat — must leave.
Int: Five working days is the minimum, but I think there's a bank holiday next week. The boat can, of course, leave as that is for the Navy to decide, but you will probably not have our responses in time. We are sure you are disappointed, but it is not just a matter of H&S — we also understand from the Research Committee that you do not have any hypotheses in your proposal — and it is its experience that most hypothesis-free research carried out by very early career researchers such as yourself is unlikely to have a major impact on the progress of science... there will be other

training opportunities for you closer to home. Have you taken the CV development course?

CD: No.

Int: Well. I suggest you go back to your room, book yourself on a few courses, and try and come up with a hypothesis and project that is a bit more feasible — remember that there is a whole section on feasibility in the on-vellum application form, and just putting 'That's up to Captain Fitzroy' is not much of an answer. And do rethink your impact statement — changing the way we look at life is really a little grandiose, and 'light will be thrown on man and his history' is just a ridiculous thing to write, don't you think?

CD: Thank you. I think I'll go and collect a few beetles from the Fens instead.

14

THE STAGES OF ACQUIESCENCE

In conversations with friends and colleagues, there is usually a consensus that life in the Ivory Flats is demanding and often unsatisfying, but the conclusion we often come to is to shrug our shoulders and have another beer or glass of wine. It is easier to just tread water, to keep afloat amid the endless managerial demands, rather than to realise the scale of change and do something about them.

This led me to thinking how we have become acquiescent to our own diminution. One aspect is obvious — we are just too busy to stand back and see what is going on, and instead we move into an entirely reactive mode.

It's impossible to start the revolution when you have 300 emails in your inbox. Lenin would never have even got to Finland Station if he had had Microsoft Exchange.

Another obvious reason is that change has been slow and incremental. I doubt any of us could put a finger on when the process started. Indeed, one would be hard put to even know exactly what the process is — is it centralisation? Bureaucratisation? Managerialism? Governmental control? And each step — a new form here, another set of guidelines there, a new level of approval everywhere — is so small that it hardly seems worth making a fuss about it.

It is reminiscent of the boiling frog syndrome — if a frog is placed in cold water, and the water gradually heated, it will not notice and not move. Small increments are imperceptible. Of course, the science of this is complete rubbish, and the frog, if it can, will leap out at the first opportunity after some level of discomfort. Perhaps frogs are smarter than lecturers, and we just did not notice enough to make the leap.

But, even if the change has been incremental, there can still be phases, not necessarily particular phases of actions taken by the University, or policies introduced, but phases in how we responded. I found that two books provide insights into the stages of acquiescence.

The first is *Watership Down*. Talking rabbits. At one level, *Watership Down*, the novel by Richard Adams published in 1972, is a children's story of talking rabbits going on an epic journey. Having left their warren because one of the rabbits foresaw its destruction (don't ask), they undergo many risks, adventures and challenges to find a new warren where they can live a wild life. Wild as in free of the farmer, rather than partying in the burrow every night. It is a gripping tale in which one soon forgets that they are talking rabbits, and sees them as heroic and occasionally tragic figures.

A children's story, but read enthusiastically by many adults, as is often the case with the best of them. But to me, it is also an allegory for the first stage of acquiescence. The novel opens with the rabbits leaving their warren as it is threatened with destruction. On their journey they join another warren, where life is comfortable and food plentiful. But there is also the shadow of fear over it.

Fiver, the rabbit with premonitions, senses death. But most of the rabbits do not want to leave this new warren, as it is comfortable and food is plentiful. Why face all the dangers of foxes and badgers and dogs, when they are well looked after here? Of course, it turns out the farmer is feeding them, but also culling them. There is a price for being well looked after.

While the rabbits do leave — after considerable debate among remainers and leavers — for more adventures in search of a home, their stay at this warren is a useful allegory for how universities have changed, and in particular, how academics have acquiesced to being looked after. In the good or bad old days, depending on your point of view, academics did most of the administration. This can take many forms, and across my career I have been secretary to many committees, written screeds of minutes, set timetables, ordered colour pens, you name it.

Most of my colleagues, except those who had been absolved by what I now understand is called learned incompetence, did the same. There were just many other day-to-day, or often term-to-term, tasks of administration that one has had to do, some challenging, some menial, some quite adventurous, even if, sadly, my excellent paper on 'Proposed changes to the second year timetable' has had little impact on my H-index. But on the whole, they didn't take that much time, and there was considerable secretarial support.

But then the farmer came along with carrots. These jobs should really be done by administrators (no more learned incompetence), releasing academics to get on with research and teaching. And who would resist such pampering? No more writing minutes, no more investing in a paper on the best use of storerooms, just deep thoughts and slick lectures. Only a fool would turn down such progress. And so it came to pass.

Admittedly, the carrots were a bit thin on the ground, and it turned out that more people were needed to deliver the few carrots, but there was a sense, and I remember it well, that somehow this was going to liberate us, make us secure. Even more, professionalism would come in to replace our amateur efforts, streamlining — bring on the efficiency — the way we operated.

Of course, it turned out to be nothing like that. While, as far as I know, there was no culling of lecturers for their meat and skin, the carrots came at a cost. Autonomy and initiative were lost, and perhaps above all else, the knowledge. Not the knowledge of how to navigate London without a sat-nav, but the knowledge of how the system worked, where the levers of power lay, who made the decisions. The beginnings of the distancing between them and us — 'don't worry, we'll look after that', rising alarmingly to 'we know best'.

A shrug of the shoulders, the urge to just get on with one's own things, and ultimately, for new academic staff, total acquiescence to their place in the system, and the assumption that their agency was restricted to writing lectures and getting grants. Not that the farmers were alone — many academics recognised that being the ones to provide the links between them and us, and to gradually morph into farmers, was the way to get on. Soon the administrators found the most efficient way to administer was to ask the academics to do the basics — fill in the time sheets, take photos of all the receipts, do the photocopying — and send them back for approval.

The second book is George Orwell's *1984*. Everyone knows the plot and characters of *1984* — Winston Smith, Julia, Big Brother, The Thought Police and Room 101. Much of *1984* has entered the public space and conversation. Many Big Brothers have been rightly or wrongly identified, and 'groupthink' is a widely used term. Room 101 became a television programme, where guests were asked to assign hated things to it.

Entirely irrelevantly, I once ran a seminar series called Room 101 — speakers had to select an idea or method or model in their field that they thought should go into Room 101. They also had the opportunity to pull out of Room 101 something that they felt had been wrongly neglected — it was a lot of fun. *1984* is a dark, often frightening picture of dystopia and totalitarianism.

I should say straight away that there is nothing dystopian and totalitarian about university life today, and while one might have issues with heads and vice-chancellors, none can really be remotely mistaken for Big Brother or Big Sister. No, the issue is again, acquiescence. Both Winston Smith and Julia are resentful of the state of affairs, and while he is ultimately prepared to do something, she is apathetic. Even Winston is cautious to an extreme. Across the whole of the society (except the proles), acceptance of one's lot — through fear and lack of thinking of what can be done — are the signatures of life in *1984* as much as the actions of the Ministry of Love.

A comparison with *1984* is perhaps a long stretch, but most academics today complain (often bitterly) about the burdens that take up so much of their time, but remain acquiescent to them. What is the point of trying to do something when the odds are so overwhelming? Even though the opportunities are there, at meetings and open discussions, few will raise their head above the parapet.

Those that do are often isolated. We are all familiar with meetings where, when the dissenter is speaking, everyone else is busy looking down at their notes, avoiding any chance of guilt by association. Or just despairing that this will make the meeting even longer and yield no results, and thinking of the inbox flooding while your colleague fights a losing battle.

There are many reasons for this. The worst might be the fear of getting into trouble, of becoming known as difficult, and so reducing chances of advancement (particularly for untenured or short-contract staff) or resources. The erosion of a sense of belonging to a peer group, wherever you lie in the university system, has certainly played a role here.

That same enhancement of a stratified hierarchy in the academic world, especially the empowerment of managers, means that for the most part things go from the top down, not from the bottom up, and this brings a concomitant sense of compliance, of obedience. 'We have to do it, I suppose, because "they" say so' is heard all too frequently in departmental corridors.

Above all, though — and this is not new, but enhanced by the new environment in which we work — is the fear of being ignorant. Most academics have been successful because we know a lot, and are also very good at finding things out — sadly, we were the school swots, probably! We like to understand how things work, whether it is the atom or the English parliament of the fourteenth century. Confidence comes from knowledge and understanding, but most of us haven't a clue about what is going on in the 'upper' levels of the university. Those of us, older, working in a much more academically-led environment, did know. Some of us think we still do know, but are usually wrong! But younger colleagues, pressured by work, life and the futile pursuit of a house they can afford to buy, do not, do not have the time to find out, and if they do, discover a labyrinth of web pages with obscure information. In the end, acquiescence becomes a survival strategy.

What to do? Let Hazel — sorry, back to the talking rabbits — be your guide. When faced with a deteriorating environment — the destruction of his warren, the culling of colleagues — he had the courage and decisiveness to stand up (in a rabbit sort of way, presumably) and act.

Courage — often the courage to appear an outlier — is the antidote to acquiescence. But not easy.

15

THE ALPHABET OF PROGRESS

There is a well-known danger that those who are beyond the first flush of youth tend to think that the world is going to the dogs. This is not a new phenomenon.

> I have many times asked myself ... the source of a certain error which, since it is committed by all the old without exception, can be believed to be proper and natural to man: namely, that they all praise the past and blame the present, revile our actions and behaviour and everything which they themselves did not do when they were young, and affirm, too, that every good custom and way of life, every virtue and, in short, all things imaginable are always going from bad to worse.

So wrote Baldassare Castiglione (great first name!) in 1528 in the *Book of the Courtier*, and it could easily be read as critique of these reflections, written nearly five hundred years prematurely.

Leaving aside the possibility that things really are getting worse, it might be a good opportunity to think how university life may actually have improved, and so, this time I shall reflect on how things are actually better.

One of the few songs I remember most of the words for is the Geordie singer Alex Glasgow's 'Socialist ABC'. 'A is for Alienation, that's made me the man that I am; B's for the Boss who's a Bastard, a bourgeois who don't give a damn; and C is for capitalism, the Boss's reactionary creed...' And so it goes. In the spirit of Alex Glasgow, here is the alphabet of progress in university life — but without the rhymes.

Academics

'A' could have stood for 'administration' but surprisingly it didn't. Instead it is the core of our institutions, the academics. If I look at the younger generations, they are generally better than the average of the past. There have always been exceptional academics, both as teachers and researchers, but the variance has almost certainly reduced, with a greater commitment and in particular, interest in the quality of both teaching and research (even if the conflict between these two does cause them a lot of stress). What is sad, and hopefully not noted by 'senior management', is that improvement has coincided with a sharp decline in their conditions of work.

Buildings

There is a case to be made against this one as the Cambridge Physics Department won many more Nobel Prizes in its appalling old buildings than in its more modern ones, but the expansion and improvement of university buildings is quite staggering — indeed, one might wish the same investment had been made in the more flesh and blood infrastructure, but I'm not in complaining mood. Not being cold and having the right labs is clearly a great improvement in life.

Conferences

The climate crisis and COVID have put a bit of a damper on this one, but cheaper travel and a more international outlook has opened up researchers of all ages to a greater range of outlooks and opportunities. Conferences, workshops, visiting positions, have taken academic discourse away from a few crusty learned societies dominated by men in suits to a much more open-minded and enjoyable world of networks, collaborations, friendships and romances.

Diversity

'D' is something of a no-brainer. Fifty years ago students and staff were much more homogenous — by gender, class and ethnicity. I can't pretend that anything in my person has contributed to this, but I have certainly been its beneficiary. I am sure there are many functional benefits of greater diversity, improving teaching and research, but we should not underestimate the fact that it is also more fun (see F).

ERC

UK researchers have been awarded €13.5 billion in grants from the European Research Council (ERC) from its inception until September 2021. This is not just an extraordinary boost to UK university research, but unlike so much funding these days it is directed at straightforward blue-skies projects — no seed-bedding, networking, or themes... just research. For a long time Brexit looked to wipe this jewel from my list of improvements, but at last, in 2023, the government saw sense and signed up again.

Fun

This, admittedly, is rather more aspirational than real. Those looking at the *soi-disant* Ivory Towers from a distance often give the impression that what they resent is that students and academics are enjoying themselves, and this is in contrast to the Real World. But learning, teaching, research should be fun, and still often is. Universities should be devoted to expanding horizons of all, and this is better done in an atmosphere of enjoyment than the hard discipline of either examination-fixation or H-index oppression. As I said, probably wishful thinking, I think the fun is still lurking there.

Google Scholar

Older readers will remember the Scientific Citation Index, vast volumes of microscopic print, listing citations for papers. Apart from the strain on the eyes, the time it took to follow up papers was inordinate. Google Scholar and other search engines have transformed our knowledge of our fields, whether finding new papers or exploring the way they have prompted further research. AI-driven engines will no doubt take this further, sometimes too imaginatively apparently, but Google Scholar is emblematic of easing the burden or research.

Harassment

This is not an easy one. Having had many colleagues over the years, I am sure that their behaviour with respect to students and colleagues has been irreproachable, but we have all heard of the ones who with impunity harassed and behaved inappropriately. It is a shame on us that often we did nothing despite the rumours, but in the end, they were usually just rumours, not evidence. That this sort of behaviour is now being brought under the spotlight is progress, although hopefully with a sensitivity that many people genuinely find their romantic partners at work — shared interests are not a bad basis for a relationship.

Internationalism

Walk into any lab, library or lecture room and there is a good chance that a conversation will be going on in another language. Of course, that would probably have been true in the eighteenth century, but the language would have been Latin. Now it might be Spanish, German or Chinese. The snacks being eaten could be samosas, nachos or sushi. In our research centre we would have parties where people would bring examples of their local food, and, given that we have had some 40 nationalities in our centre over the years, the meals were wonderful — as is the overall scientific and cultural experience.

Job talks

Definitely a two-edged sword, this one. On the one hand they are terrifying to give and often painful to listen to, but on the other they open up the appointments process, and bring it out of the rather secretive and hierarchy-based process that dominated previously.

Knowledge

Another one where the jury may still be out. I have often heard it said, and indeed probably said it myself, that students arrive with a much narrower knowledge-base than previously, and one can be shocked at things they don't know (as I am sure my supervisors were shocked by what I didn't know). However, it is also the case that the internet and digital resources generally have made it much easier to acquire knowledge, and so hopefully there is a premium to be gained from easy access to knowledge that gives a return in analytical and interpretive skills. Well, I am an optimist.

Lectures

In my first Department there was a lecturer who would bring the same yellowed and curled sheets of hand-written pages each year and start reading. At the end of the hour, they would mark the line they had reached, and leave, beginning at the next line the following week. Year after year... Lectures are definitely better!

Mobile phones

In the 'good old days' to make a phone call required ringing the switchboard (only after 1 p.m.) and asking for a call to be made. 'Is it personal?' was the inevitable response (which meant you got billed!). If you were lucky, in the next hour your phone would ring and you would be put through. If you were unlucky (or unpopular), you would never hear back from the operator. Making a call could take several days. God bless mobile phones, not just for making phone calls but for all the other things we can do — plan (and gossip) on WhatsApp, grab photos on the run, record talks, not to mention keep in contact in even remote field conditions.

Novelty

'N' is a hard consonant, replete with rather tough-sounding abstract nouns ('N' is for 'negative', after all). Novelty here could be a catch-all, but what I have in mind are the new subjects and new areas of research that are now possible, both in the sciences and the humanities. The hegemony of traditional subjects, looking down on upstarts, is hopefully much weaker. New ideas, new perspectives come from experimentation, intellectual and scientific, and while some may fall by the wayside as ephemeral and fashionable, some become the planks of progress. The problem, of course, is knowing which is which, but only an open-minded approach to novelty can provide the context for distinguishing the ephemeral from the permanent.

Outreach

There was certainly once a view that scientific and scholarly knowledge was too good to be shared widely, and what was shared should be outsourced to organisations such as the Workers' Educational Association. That is no longer the case, and outreach in all its forms — festivals of science and ideas, Twitter platforms, lifelong learning, science journalists, etc. — has shown the functionality and the fun of research and higher education in a way that will have the guardians of Ivory Towers turning in their graves, hopefully.

Photocopiers and PDFs

Change is progressive, with one form successfully replacing another. Photocopiers were a boon from the 1970s onwards, magically making material widely available to students and academics alike, and as they improved, they became wonders of speed (and places to meet people). PDFs continue the trend of the democratisation of information, even if the opportunities for a nice gossip are reduced.

Quantitative software

A bit nerdy, but... to calculate a statistical test on a large set of data by hand could take a lifetime. Calculating machines and early computers improved the lot of the scientist, but the real revolution came with freely available software packages on personal computers. I can now do in a few seconds what used to take days, and for my predecessors, months. The emergence and flourishing of R, free to all, has simultaneously brought greater equality and greater quality of science to the field.

Risk

One of my tasks as an undergraduate doing fieldwork was to back an ancient and rickety Land Rover up to a cliff on which an A-frame was precariously placed. I depended on another student to tell when I got to the cliff. This would drop a hoist to those below, a package would be attached (fossil, camping equipment), and then I would drive forward, and up would come the package. Rinse and repeat. Looking back it was horrendously dangerous (but a lot of fun). One can carp, and I do, about the greater restrictions in health and safety, but some of the things we did were pretty outlandish. Greater safety, if not universal caution, seems to be progress.

Students

That many think that today's students are not as knowledgeable (see K), prepared, or as interested as earlier generations (especially our own), is true, but this neglects the most important thing about students, which is they are annually refreshed, and provide new challenges all the time. Different backgrounds, different abilities, different interests are what refreshes teaching. Exasperating sometimes, but nearly always refreshing.

Talks

Talks (a broad mix of seminars, discussion groups, journal clubs, and so on) are a central part of academic life today, even to the extent that there may even be too many of them. But this is a great improvement from earlier times when there may be the occasional, very formal and often exclusive Department Seminar, but otherwise it was a desert. Post-COVID has added to this richness online access to high quality talks across the world. Seminars provide the experience to present, to ask questions (so nerve-racking to start with), and to get one's ahead above the parapets of our own specialities.

Universities

More of them... In the 1960s there were around 33 universities in England, a few more in Scotland, one in Wales. There are now more than 120 institutions of higher education. While one can quibble over many aspects of the expansion of higher education and the direction of travel in some ways, the fact that there are now so many more opportunities for both students and staff has to be one of the better things of modern Britain.

Vice-Chancellors

No, only joking. Probably good, bad and indifferent, as always.

Word processors

There is a booming market for portable typewriters, having the romantic glow of students in attics, novelists in Cuban bars, and explorers in tents, all living at the edge. There is a nostalgia for these machines, and certainly an earthly pleasure in the physicality of hitting the keys. But as someone who typed (very badly) their thesis and many papers with one, I bless the arrival of word processors. I can see there are downsides — word processors allow too many options to write paragraphs at random, and then reorder them so that they become more like

Lego constructions than flowing prose — but not retyping drafts from scratch is a blessing.

Alex Glasgow's alphabet ends with 'X, Y and Z, my dear daddy said, will be written on the street barricades' — and that's good enough for me too.

No doubt each of us would have our own list, both of things that are better and things that are worse, and mine is unashamedly subjective. While I would not go to the stake for any of them, I am interested to see what general patterns they expose.

The most striking for me is the number of these that are based on technology. We have become so accustomed to the presence of the hardware and software that supports us that a lot of the time we hardly notice, and simply take them for granted. In this there is nothing special about academics or university life in general, as virtually any field of life would reflect the fact, but research and education are particularly well placed to benefit from the digital technology that underlies the massive amount of information on which we depend.

Even though I know there are many costs — for example, word processors have transferred many administrative tasks from secretaries to the academics — I am not about to go and see if I can find my Olivetti Lettera 25.

The other generality is that they reflect a shift from a closed to a more open world. The internationalisation of universities, the diversity of the student base, the open conferences and talks, the growth of outreach and public dissemination, are all ways in which the walls of the cloister have been thinned if not fully removed. While there can always be strains brought about by enlarging the size and diversity of a community, these mostly settle down to the point that people cannot imagine anything different.

So despite the deep and very real concerns about many aspects of modern university life, it is important not to ignore what is good, and indeed better than before.

We are mistaken to think of golden ages and declinism. Each age has elements that are golden, and others that are rusty iron bars, and we should learn to keep the former and lose the latter, and certainly not, as often happens, go and look for new rusty bars. It can be that things are getting better and worse at the same time.

And as I look at my alphabet, I am struck by two things. One is that change (for the better and worse) is driven to a very large extent by factors that go way beyond the academy, and our level of agency is limited. The other, to me not surprisingly, is how virtually none of the improvements have come from top-down planning and 'senior management'. So, let's raise a glass to the improvements there have been in academic life, for which the most appropriate toast is 'Bottoms up'.

16

WE'RE ALL DOOMED... OR ARE WE?

Responses to *Notes from Ivory Flats* are often 'yes, that's exactly what it's like', which is an excellent gateway to a joint moan about the current state of British universities. These conversations often end with a question — 'But what can we do about it?'

It is all very well diagnosing the problem, but we would be pretty disappointed with a doctor who then said 'Well, you're sick, but I've really no idea what to do... Good luck!'

I don't have much of an idea, and certainly no silver bullets, but I think there are strategies of survival that can bring a bit more control, perhaps even joy, to our working lives.

I will start by introducing a new classification of academics — 'institution burrowers' and 'institution surfers'. Burrowers — more positively called institution builders — are those who see their universities (or more locally their departments) as integral to their work and that investment in their activities and development — sometimes known as improvement — are mutually beneficial. They are prepared to burrow into the depths or their institutions to affect how they work.

As an inveterate institution burrower myself, there is great satisfaction in developing new courses and new course structures, building research groups and centres, organising seminars, and having a say in the running of our place of work. It is well known that one of the main drivers of job satisfaction lies in having a sense of control. There is also the ability to influence the direction of travel, although in my case, I felt I was often the buffers over which the runaway train ran. I think above all, though, the pleasure of being a burrower lies in the interactions with colleagues, other academics, administrators, and students who felt they were part of a shared journey.

Surfers are those who see their institution as, at best, a useful vehicle for their own career, and at worst an address of convenience. Many are self-identified superstars. Surfers glide along the surface of the institution, barely getting a foot wet in the sea of work that running the institution involves. Some are perennially at conferences, but most are just experts at keeping their heads down when volunteers are sought or duties are assigned. Some have learned incompetence, while others are simply 'too busy'. The true experts are those who take on the duties and then manage to delegate them to others.

It is a sad fact that surfers are often promoted ahead of burrowers, as they do find time to write grants and publish prolifically. And much of what I have written about in these notes could certainly imply that we should all be surfers now.

As managerialism takes over, why burrow when the administration can do it for you, leaving you to surf to your heart's content? And that might be one answer to my question — what can be done? Let it go. In the downward spiral that many of us see in British university life, being a burrower is a bit of a dead-end niche.

But I think this is a mistake, and in fact many of the colleagues I have known over the years remain committed to investing in their institution. Despite my criticisms, university life remains broadly pleasurable, and despite the growing tensions, we want to make it better. If we want to preserve what is good, we must be involved. This is not a case of using our badger-like claws to hold up change, but to shape it, through both resistance and initiative.

So, as an optimist, the question for me is how, not if. Before making some suggestions, I would stress a caveat. The symbiotic bond between university and individual academics has morphed from strong mutualism to a more unbalanced one.

This is not a reason for not investing and burrowing, but for being aware of the limits, to not be naïve in believing that one's efforts are appreciated, and to set firm boundaries where one does not lose sight of one's own teaching and research interests and work-life balance. Too many people are like the Marlon Brando character in *On the Waterfront* — 'I could have been a contender'. They could have submitted that grant, they could have published those results first, but they didn't have time due the commitments on the graduate appeals committee, the space allocation working party, their pastoral activities...

University life is a trade-off, and one should always keep an eye on where one's own interests lie in that trade-off, between investment and commitment to one's institution, ultimately the basis for our success and working happiness, and personal achievement in our fields of research. Managers may have a different view on that trade-off.

So now we are really prepared to ask — what should one do? First, one must know how the system works. This used to be a case of reading big books full of ordinances and regulations, and talking to people (secretaries were particularly good here). University mechanics are much more fluid and opaque now, with information buried in websites, emails, Teams, and the ether generally.

Directives and changes also come down at a much greater speed, so just keeping up is a daunting task — 'Ah yes, that was last year's risk assessment form, this year's has been completely changed...' Indeed, keeping up is probably a task that is incompatible with doing much else, or one's sanity. But it is worth a try, as only by knowing what is going on can one hope to have an effect. Too often, by the time you have discovered that all lectures will be automatically recorded and captioned by a bot, it is too late to stop such madness.

Knowing what is going on is, however, only half the battle. Most universities, and especially Oxford and Cambridge, operate through a committee system. There are formally composed committees, such as Faculty Boards or School Councils (or other such appropriately named), and traditionally decisions and accountability lies with them. Old hands knew how to burrow through minutes to find out exactly what decision had been formally made, and can distinguish between those and just statements of intent or hope with no authority.

This is phenomenally dull, and has more than a whiff of antiquarianism. However, it meant that there was a level of transparency and accountability. Increasingly though, such formal committees are bypassed and supplanted by *ad hoc* ones, such as 'executive committees', 'management teams', even 'senior management teams', and by administrative division directors, assistant directors, deputy assistant directors (or do I mean assistant deputy directors?). This makes searching for the locus of decision making like searching for the yeti.

An impossible task, and giving up is the obvious option. But I think there is a shortcut, and that is just to ask — 'where is this proposal/decision/directive coming from?' In effect, this is searching for the elusive 'they' or even the more apparently authoritative 'The University'. 'Who are "they?"' should be tattooed on the hands of every lecturer and professor.

There is another way. These could be criticised for 'othering' administrators and managers, and in doing so not giving respect to people who are working hard and are committed to their goals. And I'm sure it works the other way too.

For years, I worked with a technician who would invariably leave a room with a *sotto voce* 'bloody academics', and I am sure that anthem can be heard in central administrations all over the world. The important thing, though, is to get to know the people you work with, even if they are remote. COVID and remote working, not to mention the centralisation of administration, has made personal contact optional and minimal, and that can only create misunderstandings.

Both sides — and I am doing it again by calling it both sides —need to get out there and mingle, not just on a once-a-year garden party, but day-to-day contact. Bring back the phone, and bring back the dropping in. Bring back the gossip, the light-hearted chats about nothing much, for these become the building blocks of trust. Bring back proximity of offices. Make friends. There is much to be learnt and gained. Shared relationships bring shared understanding. We are a social species, not a digital one — or at least, not yet!

Making friends can be put more pragmatically — make networks of people you know across all levels. COVID and centralisation have limited personal networks. It used to be the case that it was relatively easy to have a network of people you knew across many parts of the university system, across many ages.

It is my sense that this is harder now, and the networks are smaller and overlap less. This is partly a result of the growth of hierarchies and lines of management, but it is worth making the effort to cut across these, and with this will come shared information, shared interests, and a greater sense of empowerment and influence, no matter where you lie in the system. This, of course, takes energy, initiative, and overcoming that awful sense of shyness that is an integral part of any British institution.

I think ignorance of what is going on lies at the root of many problems — any economist or military general will tell you of the dangers of incomplete information. The multiple types of silos that now exist in university life only enhance the lack of shared knowledge.

This is compounded by the sense that you are the only one thinking some heretical thought, and the foundation of groupthink and acquiescence. Fear of being a lone voice based on ignorance of what others think and how the system works is a powerful force. What is surprising is how often, when one does speak up, others will come up to you afterwards and say 'that's exactly what I was thinking'.

Having networks that you have built provides you with the armour to say what you think, and to challenge authority, and so become an effective burrower rather than one who gets buried as the tunnel collapses.

But why bother, you might well ask? Why not just surf and get a better suntan? Bizarrely, I would turn here to the military. When soldiers have done something of enormous bravery, and won a great medal, they are asked if they did it for King and Country in a fervour of patriotic enthusiasm. Invariably the reply is, no, of course not, 'I did it for my mates'.

And we should do it for our mates, be they students, colleagues, collaborators, early career researchers, even competitors as we need them too, and especially for those coming after us. There may never have been a golden age of universities and academic life, for each generation faced challenges and conflicts, but there is little doubt that there was much that was of value in the freer and more democratic academic world that my generation benefitted from, and preserving and restoring that is worth a bit of burrowing.

NOTES

1. A change of address

1. Francis M. Cornford (1922) *Microcosmographia Academica: Being a Guide for the Young Academic Politician*. Bowes and Bowes, Cambridge.

2. How old is The University?

1. Eric Blair, Last man in the university: it's 13 o'clock on campus, *Times Higher Education*, 7 April 2016.

4. Why we are all folding napkins now

1. Steve Jobs, *The Lost Interview* (2012).

6. Forget the time management courses, ask the peahen

1.https://hbr.org/2019/01/how-to-spend-way-less-time-on-email-every-day

7. When actions speak louder than organograms

1. From Isaiah Berlin's essay 'The Fox and the Hedgehog', and before that, the Greek poet Archilochus — a fox knows many things, a hedgehog one important thing.
2. John Ross, Many masters, few functionaries as professional ranks transform, *Times Higher Education*, 25 November 2020.
3. *Cambridge University Reporter*, No 6587, 29 July 2020.

11. Fearful asymmetry: the end of the peer show

1.https://researchbriefings.files.parliament.uk/documents/SN04252/SN04252.pdf
2. David Bogle (2018) 100 Years of the PhD in the UK. In: *Proceedings of Vitae Researcher Development International Conference 2018, Birmingham, UK.* Careers Research and Advisory Centre (CRAC) Limited.
3. R. Dawkins and J. R. Krebs, Arms Races between and within Species. *Proceedings of the Royal Society of London. Series B, Biological Sciences*, 21 Sep. 1979, Vol. 205, No. 1161, pp. 489–511.

12. The great university subsidy scandal

1.https://ec.europa.eu/eurostat/statistics-explained/index.php? title=Hours_of_work_-_annual_statistics#How_does_the_average_working_week_vary_across_economic_activities_and_occupations.3F

13. Are you sure that boat is safe, Mr Darwin?

1. Peter Raby (2001) *Alfred Russel Wallace: a Life*. Princeton.
2. Janet Browne (1996) *Charles Darwin: Voyaging*. Pimlico.
3. Richard Slobodin (1997) *W.H.R. Rivers: Pioneer Anthropologist, Psychiatrist of the Ghost Road*. Sutton.
4. He did.
5. Health & Safety may have been right on this one. It has been suggested that Chagas disease was responsible for many of Darwin's subsequent health problems.
6. Darwin witnessed the eruption of the Osorno volcano in the Andes while in Chile.
7. Darwin experienced the earthquake that Valdivia in Chile; the earthquake destroyed the town of Concepción.
8. Darwin took part in a mission with 50 armed men to retake a mutinous garrison; he experienced a number of other violent political upheavals. He was excited about 'Pistols and Cutlass'.

Printed in Great Britain
by Amazon

2faa22bc-293b-464e-8012-53efbd2f472eR01